LITERACY FOR ALL CHILDREN

A FORMULA FOR LEAVING NO CHILD BEHIND

Carolyn McKenzie Lawrence

6/26/04

To Walt & Victoria,
Thank you for being
the special people you are
love
Carolyn

ScarecrowEducation
Lanham, Maryland • Toronto • Oxford
2004

Published in the United States of America
by ScarecrowEducation
An imprint of The Rowman & Littlefield Publishing Group, Inc.
4501 Forbes Boulevard, Suite 200, Lanham, Maryland 20706
www.scarecroweducation.com

PO Box 317
Oxford
OX2 9RU, UK

British Library Cataloguing in Publication Information Available

Library of Congress Cataloging-in-Publication Data

Lawrence, Carolyn M.
  Literacy for all children : a formula for leaving no child behind /
Carolyn McKenzie Lawrence.
    p. cm.
  ISBN 1-57886-105-5 (pbk. : alk. paper)
  1. Elementary school principals—United States—Anecdotes. 2. School
management and organization—United States—Anecdotes. 3. Reading
(Elementary)—United States. I. Title.
LB2831.92 .L39 2004
372.12'012—dc22   2003023550

∞™ The paper used in this publication meets the minimum requirements of
American National Standard for Information Sciences—Permanence of Paper
for Printed Library Materials, ANSI/NISO Z39.48-1992.
Manufactured in the United States of America.

To Gordon D. Lawrence, Ph.D.,
husband, mentor, editor, and friend.

In memory of Mary H. McCaulley, Ph.D., cofounder of
the Center for Applications of Psychological Type (CAPT).

CONTENTS

Acknowledgments   vii

1   Why This Book?   1

2   Making School a Personal Place to Be   15

3   Discipline   39

4   Ironing Out Our Expectations
     for Instruction   67

5   Ramifications of Poverty   99

6   Getting Rid of Bad Teaching and
     Supporting Good Teaching   117

7   Reflections   139

About the Author   141

ACKNOWLEDGMENTS

I'd like to thank the following people for their assistance: James T. Castellow, P.E., James R. Davis, P.E., William D. Hedges, Ph.D., Ann W. Hedman, M.ED., Edna S. McCown, Ph.D., Nancy F. McKenzie, Ph.D., and Jeanne A. Myrick.

1

WHY THIS BOOK?

This book has several purposes. Its overriding purpose is to give you a personal account, with stories, about how children can be successful in school every day. Children are our focus in education. Yet, under the pressure of test scores, accountability, and school ratings, we are forgetting what is in the best interest of each and every child. Because of this, sadly, many decisions about schooling are made for political reasons and may not be what is in the best interests of children. This is especially true of decisions made about instruction.

All the years of K–12 education are crucial. Yet the most important years for catching children's interest and keeping children committed to the arduous process of education are the very early years. A child's love of learning should be kindled very early on, from birth through about third grade.

Each child in the primary grades *must* succeed every day. This is necessary for all children to develop academically, socially, and physically. It is even more essential for children who come to school with self-esteem problems or who, early on in their school years, quickly recognize that they are behind other children academically. We know from the research literature that 75 percent of achievement in academics is based on a child's self-esteem as a learner. If a child can succeed early in education, then chances are very good that the child will successfully complete the K–12 process.

Daniel is a highly active child who comes to school happy and enthusiastic about learning. He hops into the kindergarten classroom that first week, a blonde, beautiful five-year-old who is very outgoing. During the first week, Daniel listens to the other children recite nursery rhymes with the teacher and identify colors and letters on a page. Daniel does not know nursery rhymes, colors, or letters, and this upsets him.

Although Daniel's mother is affluent, she has never taken the time to read extensively to Daniel, to teach him that letters and sounds make words and, therefore, are a means of communication. Daniel is the product of a single-parent home, a father he has never met, and a mother focused on her career.

Daniel is an only child, loved by his mother and maternal grandparents, and he has been spoiled by them. He has never been taught acceptable behavior. When he is in the outside world, if he does not get his way he throws a tantrum and embarrasses his mother or grandparents. They cope with Daniel by giving him what he wants. Daniel is a very loving child who frequently hugs and wants to please, but he is ostracized by neighbors and other children because of his behavior. His behavior is not his fault; it is the fault of a parent who would not take the time to train Daniel.

In the classroom, within the first week, Daniel becomes a terrible problem for the teacher. He screams when he does not get what he wants and tears his papers into shreds because he does not know how to do the work. Daniel is on a road to disaster and is quickly developing poor self-esteem in relation to schoolwork.

The teacher has the burden of correcting his behavior and, at the same time, helping him learn what the other children already know. Daniel needs to be given work on his own instructional level so that he can learn about colors, numbers, and sounds. Daniel is called *developmentally low*. He has an above-average IQ but is behind the rest of the class. Daniel first needs to learn about rules and what constitutes acceptable social behavior. Then the teacher must find a way to give him success every day in what he is attempting to learn.

The kindergarten teacher has this problem with Daniel and knows that she has to address his deficiencies while still motivating the other children. We know that most kindergarten classrooms have at least six instructional levels per class. It is likely that Daniel's teacher has to deal with three or four other troubled children and their different instructional levels.

In many ways, Daniel is lucky. He is wanted by his grandparents, has enough to eat, has a secure home environment, and can learn easily. But he is abused in the sense that his mother is too busy for him and has not taken the time to teach him correct social behavior. Other even more needy children are more threatened than Daniel. Some have never held a book. These children cannot survive in our school system without having success every day. Their success in life, literally, depends on what a teacher can do for them early in the educational process.

There is a great need to put more decisions about instruction in the hands of teachers and the network of people associated with each school and each child. I hope that after you read this book you will have a much clearer picture of public education. I hope that you will be motivated to ask the educators in your local school how you can help put children's needs, instead of test scores, back into the center of our educational process and how you can be a mentor to one of these children needing extra help in the early grades.

For those educators and parents who want to know how to improve instruction in a school, I have filled the book with examples of what works and what does not work. In the last twenty years of my thirty-three-year career, I worked in schools that served poverty-ridden neighborhoods. The descriptions and stories here are about the angles we worked, the shortcuts we used, the deals we dealt, and the risks we took in making a learning community for our children. This book is about the instructional heart of the elementary school and what is needed to make it vital and responsive to each child.

My intention also is to make you laugh, maybe cry, and understand how much *soul* it takes to teach and be a part of our public schools. While negative press is raging about schools, our society needs to see the constructive things that are happening daily to our children in public education.

The stories in this book really happened. Whole conversations and situations came back to me as I reviewed my daily notes. These notes, taken in steno pads for six years, helped keep me on track as a principal. I walked around the campus; met with teachers, children, and parents; and made lists of jobs to do. The notes contain many stories. I would like to make you a participant in them in order to give you an insider's view of the schooling process. I especially hope that school principals will read this book as a source of ideas for making improvements in instruction at their schools, aiming toward instruction that emphasizes successful reading and self-esteem for every child.

THE PROBLEM OF CORRECT INSTRUCTIONAL LEVEL

As I contemplated how to start this book, I was reminded of Sarah, a migrant child who was at a low level developmentally. I found her in my first classroom visit as a new principal. I quietly walked into a kindergarten room with my "Just Visiting" badge. Immediately I saw a little girl sitting in a corner, all alone. She was unkempt, with a dirty, tear-streaked face. I walked over to speak to her. The teacher, giving the class instructions to keep working at their seats, whispered to me: "Sarah absolutely refuses to do her work! This is work I *know she can do if she would*! She is to write in the numbers to ten, and she just scribbled all over her paper with black crayon. Look at this messy paper." I asked if I might take Sarah to the office. I borrowed counting chips, a duplicate math page, and a pencil.

As we walked to the office, I told Sarah: "You know, sometimes school just seems too hard. But maybe if you and I work together, we can make it a little easier for you and find out what is happening." She looked at me pitifully. Her whole body language showed defeat and hopelessness.

When we got into my office, I took the counting chips and began: "We are going to play a game and see how many numbers you know." I reached for a kindergarten math book I had in my instructional supplies and pulled out a page that requires a child to identify objects and tell the quantity of each group of objects. (Starting below the level that the teacher had required gave Sarah a chance to be successful and gave me a chance to see what she knew.)

"Let's see, Sarah. First, I want you to help me count these chips. Let's see [putting out one], how many is this?" Sarah mumbled, "One." "Great, now see there, you do know some of your numbers. How many are these? [I put out three]." Sarah counted, "One, two, uh, four?" "Four?" I said: "Do we have four?" She said, "Yes."

"Okay, Sarah. Look at me. Now, without looking at your paper or the counters, I want you to just count to ten for me out loud. Look at my face. Now, like, one, two. Now you do it." Sarah said, "One, two, uh, three, uh, four. Ten." "That's *right*! Now, let's look at the counters again." I took three counters and put them down for her to see. "Count these for me just like you are counting to ten for me out loud."

I began, "This is [I put down one]," and she said: "One." "Right—that's just right. Now, how many is this? [I put down two.] Start with one and then count the counters. Like this, one [I pointed to one], two [I pointed to the second one], and then one more." I pointed to the third one.

Sarah straightened herself in the chair and with a great deal of concentration said, "One [pointing to the first counter], two [pointing to the second counter], four [pointing to the third counter]." "No, Sarah, you are saying: 'One, two, four.' Now watch my face, and let's count together to ten again. One, two, and what comes after two?" She said, *"Three!"* and beamed with delight.

"Yes! Sarah, you see what you are doing? You are remembering to count the counters just like you remembered to count to ten. I want you to tell me exactly how many counters are on the table now." She said, *"Three!"*

I gave her a big hug and said, "That's right, three! Now aren't you smart? See, you are learning three today!" She began to blossom and smile and seemed ready to work some more. "Now we need to take this paper, and we need to put the numbers into the boxes to show you know how many are here. One, two, and three—do you know how to make a one?" She made a one on the top of the paper for me. "Can you make a two?" She made a two, but it was backward.

We worked for several minutes on how to make a two, and then I pointed to the square on the paper that had three ducks in it. I said: "Now Sarah, how many ducks do you see?" She very laboriously pointed and counted, "One, two, uh, *three!*" "Yes, Sarah, you are right! Are you smart or what?!" She clapped her hands, straightened her posture, beamed, and said, "Yes!"

I put "100" for a grade at the top of the paper and said, "I want your teacher to see this 100 you made on your paper!" (Actually, my goal was to have the teacher see that Sarah could not possibly have done the seat work given to her that morning.) Sarah said, "Can I have a happy face?" I realized my mistake, that she did not yet recognize a grade of 100 in kindergarten, and I said, "Of course you can!" and drew her a happy face.

"Let's just try a little bit more." We spent about fifteen minutes differentiating among one, two, and three by counting objects on several pages I had torn from a workbook. After I was sure she could tell one, two, and three apart, I pulled out a paper that had between one and four objects. Pointing to a box that had four objects, I said, "Sarah, count and tell me how many are in this box." Very laboriously she counted, "One, two, three, and, uh, a *thousand* of 'em!" I laughed and gave her a big hug! "No, Sarah, that's not a thousand, but aren't you smart for learning the numbers to three today?"

On her paper I wrote her teacher a note saying: "Sarah now knows her numbers to three. We had to learn the number three today with 'one-to-one correspondence.' She can count to ten but definitely does not know quantities to ten. Thanks for lending her to me—she really wants to please you." I gave Sarah a big hug and said, "Now, you see how smart you are? I want you to take this to your teacher, with these counters, and give her your paper." Sarah smiled and replied, "And can I tell her how smart I am?" I gave her another hug and said, "Of course!"

PRINCIPAL AS CLASSROOM PARTICIPANT

This episode emphasized to me, once again, how critical it is for principals to get into classrooms informally and frequently. Although making time for classroom visiting is difficult, I know that principals can spot these kinds of problems. This book tells how to identify children's difficulties and how to build an atmosphere where children's daily success is the focus and where test scores are a secondary product of successful learning, as they should be.

If a principal can spend an hour each day in the classrooms, then the whole school can focus on success for every child. But the principal has to set the tone by being in the classroom and helping with instruction. Then the entire school knows where the priorities lie for the administration. All teachers need this kind of interaction with their principal about instruction. They also feel much more supported when the principal sees them often and relates to their difficult job.

In this book I tell how I was able, as a new principal, to set up this "hands-on" approach with teachers and children. I give specific guidelines for helping a principal target one area of instruction (reading) and focus on this area for a few years. I know that this approach works. In our school the average of our test scores in all areas of achievement—not just in reading—went up with this approach.

THE INSTRUCTIONAL HEART OF THE SCHOOL

This is a foundation chapter. In it I want to show how I formed my view of instruction and why it is central to the whole process of school leadership. I was blessed in my career by being introduced to a clear picture of instruction in my undergraduate teacher preparation program—a viewpoint that became clearer, richer, deeper, and more powerful through the years as I gained on-the-job experience. Essentially, the goal is to connect with each child on his or her specific instructional level every day, at least in reading, so that the child can experience daily success. The whole school effort is then built around that goal. In the stories here, you will see how I and others worked to carry this ideal into reality.

I have also included here a longer story to show how instruction and the social-emotional climate of the school are intertwined. When I moved to Florida as a young teacher I was assigned a first grade class. I found that children at my new school were from much poorer homes than at the schools where I did my first six years of teaching in Atlanta. Instruction in first grade was easy for me when the children had parents who coached them at home. When I went to the first faculty meeting at my new school, I was given a class list with section number 1- 6. I asked my grade chairperson, "What does Section 1- 6 mean?" Her answer was that the children were grouped by ability and that I had the lowest of six first grade groups. In Florida, in the 1960s, these children had not had kindergarten or day care and were grouped by ability as identified by a screening test.

The other teachers and I spent several days preparing for the school year. We created our lesson plans and got materials and supplies for the children. The district gave us a list of skills and objectives that were to be taught the first twelve weeks of school.

MY FIRST SIX WEEKS

Within the first week with my students, I realized that we would have to work on skills far more simple and basic than those on the district's list of objectives. Frowns had appeared on the children's faces when they attempted simple letter- or color-recognition tasks. When we worked on picture books of nursery rhymes, they had no clue about rhyming words and were truly baffled about most of the foundation skills I was trying to teach.

By having a parent volunteer come and read to the class, I was freed to carefully screen each child. I found that most of them were at least two years behind in prerequisite skills—the skills needed as a foundation for academic reading and math. This lack of prerequisite skills did not mean that the children were less bright than the other first grade children. Even though they were labeled as being at a low level, this label came from their lack of experience with books, coordination tasks, listening, and knowing how to share, which necessitated placement behind other first grade children.

In two days, I had the testing data completed. I regrouped the materials and gathered new ones, and we began learning our first and most important preliminary skill: the ability to listen. For thirty minutes each morning, I played a *listening* record, and the children identified the sounds of airplanes taking off, cars honking, and dogs barking. I knew that the children, by learning to listen, could take the next step in learning to discriminate the sounds of letters. Listening is *truly* an essential skill that must be taught daily and is often neglected early in the educational process.

For the correct instructional level in language development, the children needed to learn to speak in complete sentences. When a child answered a question, I helped him or her recognize complete sentences by using a complete sentence. If I asked the question, "What did you have for breakfast this morning?" they had to answer using a complete sentence—"I had cereal for breakfast this morning"—as opposed to their normal reply, which would be, "Cereal." (Currently, broadening oral language skills such as this is being recognized as important at all grade levels.)

In addition to basic oral language development, skills prerequisite to math, reading, and writing had to be developed. These children also lacked large and small motor coordination skills. Whole body balance is very important for being able to graduate to reading from left to right and other basic reading skills. To help develop eye–hand coordination and left-to-right orientation, I laid a 2' × 4' plank on the floor and had the students walk on it as a balance beam each time they lined up to leave the classroom. At recess, we practiced eye–hand coordination activities, such as bouncing a ball and catching it. All these skills are prerequisite skills to "average" first grade work.

DAVID: GETTING TO THE PREREQUISITES

My favorite example and most needy student, in regard to eye–hand coordination, is David! David is a tall, thin child who has only one large tooth in the front of his mouth. This tooth is a novelty when he smiles, and he smiles *all the time*. He literally skips (or stumbles) into the room with a huge smile on his face *every* morning. He loves being in this new, exciting environment with all his new friends. He is very social, naive, and developmentally slow. He cannot manage to hold a pencil or crayon effectively. He can, however, use chalk to make large strokes on the chalkboard in practicing writing.

David is a major blessing to our class because he shows uninhibited love for everyone. When he fails to perform a task the other children can easily do, he smiles and laughs at himself, thus softening the embarrassment of other children when they cannot perform. He creates a climate of gentleness in the classroom that is amazing and helpful to us all.

To further develop eye–hand coordination, at recess we practice the skill of catching a ball on the first bounce. Each time the ball is bounced to David, he is always late in reacting as the ball sails by him. Never once does he show discouragement as he happily retrieves the ball and throws it back (usually in the general direction of the circle).

After a couple of weeks, all the other children in the classroom have mastered this skill. They are allowed to go to the playground equipment while I work solely with David. After three days he is finally able to catch the ball on the first bounce. As he lines up to go inside, beaming from ear to ear, he tells the class. The whole class spontaneously claps for David.

Toward the end of the school year, the whole class erupts again with glee when David is able to write his name (a foot high) on the chalkboard. We all celebrate!

Surprisingly, David is not burdened with low self-esteem, the biggest obstacle to children's learning. This emotional barrier to school learning emerges in the first school year with the expectation that every child will begin learning the same skills, no matter what previous experiences he or she has had. In my new school, the school district's achievement expectations for first grade were the same for all children—irrespective of their skill differences upon entering school, which had been identified by the screening test. We know that children develop in spurts and at different rates. When children learn to walk, we seldom chastise a slower infant. Instead, we encourage and encourage, until the feat is accomplished. Learning to read is every bit as difficult as learning to walk. Why can't we give children time to develop as they need to develop?

MY FIRST BUREAUCRATIC OBSTACLE

After the first six weeks of school, our chairperson, Betty, says that she needs to report to the district how many students are earning grades A, B, C, D, and F in reading. At the grade meeting, she begins by asking the teacher of Section 1-1 to call out the number and the grade. The teacher replies that all her children, not surprisingly, are in the A category. The meeting progresses, and as the section numbers go higher, the grades of the children get lower. By Section 1- 4 there are several Fs, meaning "failure" in learning to master the reading skills. Then it is my turn.

I inform her that my children are mostly in the A category but that I have a few in the B category. Startled, the other five teachers exclaim: "That's impossible!" "What in the world do you mean? That's ridiculous—you have the low group." "Your children can't be more successful than the higher sections! What will the parents say?"

Startled and perplexed, I say, "The parents? I don't understand." Betty explains that many of the parents in our community compare the grade sections, and the specific grade in reading, of their children with those of the other children in the neighborhood. They know exactly which children are "labeled" Section 1- 5 or 1- 6 (the low groups). The fact that my children (Section 1- 6) are getting a higher grade than the ones with higher ability would be a problem with the parents in the neighborhood.

I reply that I am sorry but that I refuse to give my children Fs based on the academic ability of other children—just because they are in the same *age* category for first grade. Each child in my class, I explain, is working to capacity. Admittedly, they are not academically where most of the upper sections are, but I have not expected them to be. I tell them that I have discovered some major readiness problems in these children, which are not their fault. I will not damage their self-esteem by giving them low grades for hard work!

The other teachers are unsettled. They say that I am not following district guidelines and that I am endangering the integrity of school practices that have been followed for many years. The rest of the first grade staff is in agreement that I am treading on dangerous and unchartered territory. Dismayed, I plead for all of us to have a conference with the principal.

At that meeting, I explain that I would like to use the process of learning to read as my example of how we might be damaging children. Because reading is the core of primary-grade teaching and is the most difficult task in primary grades for some children, this seems a good place to start. Learning to read is the basis of most successful instruction in other subjects.

I tell the teachers and the principal that readiness for reading is very similar to teeth appearing in a young child's mouth. We do not expect all children's teeth to come in at the same age of one, two, or three years. We do not call a child slow because one child has four teeth and another, the same age, has ten. The same could be said for the reading process. We *must* not penalize children by expecting them to grasp all the symbols and abstractions of learning to read by a particular time. Irrespective of intelligence, some children are more capable of coping with the abstract symbols than others. Others have had disadvantaged early childhoods. An F is devastating to any child and parent, especially on the *first* report card, which is so early in the academic career. The *joy* of learning to read is the goal here, not comparing children's abilities at five or six years old!

Fortunately for me, the principal allows us to compromise on the established grading system. I am not required to give any of my children an F in reading. In the space provided for a grade, we put both the section and the grade on the report card. First the section number appears, then the grade for reading. That means that I can put "Level 6/A" on the report card. This is enough of a concession for me and still distinguishes, for the parents, which section their child is in and how he or she is doing compared with other children. (The impact of parents on our public grading system is still as profound today as it was thirty years ago. Our system still demands distinguishing among children, to the children's detriment.) Although this compromise is not a perfect solution in my eyes, at least my children have a *chance* of developing good self-esteem about their learning ability.

EARLY CHILDHOOD AFFECTS READING ABILITY

Permit me a side comment about my own early childhood. My four sisters and I were excellent readers and enthusiastic learners. When I reflected on my childhood experiences in Atlanta, I realized that many of my play activities as a young child enhanced my coordination and readiness for reading. Both of my parents were working parents and, although not affluent, were very intelligent and educated.

There were many opportunities for my sisters and me to develop the prerequisite skills for reading. With neighborhood friends in our Atlanta community we talked as we walked to the neighborhood school. We played games in the evenings (kick the can; one, two, three, red light!; and hide-and-seek). We walked on sidewalk curbs (akin to the balance beam), sorted and played marbles, swapped trinkets from a penny machine, collected and swapped comic books, sold lemonade, and skated in the streets in front of our houses. In those days of quieter streets, we had a safe environment in which to develop the motor coordination skills that come from active physical play.

These activities developed large- and small-muscle coordination, balance, and eye–hand coordination. Our social skills were enhanced and our vocabularies were broadened because of our contact with ten to twelve children every day.

Balance and eye–hand coordination are a must for being able to scan a page and locate a first word and for picture–word association. Motor coordination develops the ability to concentrate, hold and use a pencil, and develop positive self-esteem, among many other things.

These advantages, plus the incredibly important advantage of having parents who valued reading, made us successful in school. We learned the love of reading from our parents' example. Having time to read quietly each night was a major treat to my parents and gave us impetus very early in life to work out glitches in learning to read so that we could be part of the family ritual. We all wanted to be a part of the experience.

Sadly, many children do not have the advantages of learning from each other in play (which is a wonderful and much more natural way to develop) or being read to for stimulation and recreation. In seeing our parents and older siblings loving to read and learn, we strove individually to be successful.

MY SECOND BUREAUCRATIC OBSTACLE

By the end of this first school year in Florida, all my children have made good academic progress based on individual development levels. But according to district guidelines, I am required to retain or "fail" seventeen of my children because they did not meet the district standards of skill achievement required to enter second grade. Sick at heart, once again, I approach the principal.

"Please, Mr. Myrick, would you allow me to move with my students to second grade next year? I really would like to *pass* all my children this year. I feel these children are making tremendous progress. I don't want to fail them. With another year, I truly believe they will be successful and capable of doing third grade work."

Bless his heart, although setting a precedent in this school, he allowed these seventeen children to move to second grade with me. During the summer additional new children were assigned to me to make the second grade sections even in number. The other children in my original class, who were able to meet the first grade objectives, were given to another teacher in second grade.

Having taught these seventeen *developmentally low* students for a full year proves to be wonderfully constructive as we enter their second grade year. By the end of the second grade, the children are independent, enthusiastic readers and confident students. Some are a little lower than "average" according to district guidelines, but all seventeen meet the criteria to move to the third grade.

Three years later, I am working in my new position as a curriculum resource teacher in another poverty area. I am called to the office and asked to screen a student who transferred to our school. There sits Tracey, one of my former *developmentally low* students from my other school. I am delighted to see this former student. I do a quick reading screening on Tracey, now in the fifth grade, for her new teacher and find that she is *on level* in reading. Yes!

Several weeks later, her cumulative folder arrives. I find that Tracey has been an honor student for the last year. She had no lingering effects of being labeled developmentally low in the first grade and especially enjoys reading! I say to myself, "How wonderful to see that one of those children has made progress and climbed out of the 'track' that may have limited her through all her school experience."

In my thirty-two years in public education, I have found a basic truth for success in elementary school. No matter what my job description—teacher, reading specialist, resource teacher, assistant principal, or principal—I found that teaching each child on the correct developmental or instructional level in reading is the most essential ingredient for developing and cementing his or her self-esteem and successful learning skills. The correct instructional level in the classroom is the foundation for maintaining good discipline. To have a child read successfully is the single most important aspect of learning and discipline in the primary grades. Learning to read is also the single most important factor in keeping children physically or mentally from dropping out of school.

SUMMARY OF CHAPTERS

In chapter 2, I tell you about the mind-set I brought to my new school, my priorities, and my experiences getting to know the faculty and facilities before the start of the new school year. Our discipline process proved very effective in maintaining a smooth-running campus, as shown in chapter 3 and throughout the book. Reducing discipline problems to a minimum is essential for freeing the principal's time—time needed to get into classrooms and start the serious work on instructional leadership. Good discipline schoolwide is the foundation of good instruction.

Chapter 4 is about issues involved when a principal initially begins to assist teachers and sees what is happening in the classrooms. Specific instances and stories give the reader ideas of how to enlist faculty commitment to improvements, especially in reading instruction. Chapter 5 is about the complications from poverty that many children brought to our school and how they can be minimized during school hours. Specific stories of success (and failure) are included, with guidelines for improving communication with parents, health services, and district staff.

Marginal and incompetent teachers are the focus of chapter 6. Through stories about individual teachers, I show what is involved in helping those who can improve and working through a dismissal process for those who cannot or will not improve to an acceptable level. The summary chapter includes a listing of what I as a principal had success with and what I would do better if I had a chance to start afresh.

2

MAKING SCHOOL A PERSONAL PLACE TO BE

MY RATIONALE

In my twenty years of being in public education prior to being a principal, I had seen many variables beyond the teachers' control that were detrimental to children's love of learning. The diminished freedom of the teacher, negative press raging almost daily, standardized tests not well matched to the curriculum, and decisions being made by educators and politicians who do not know the research on effective teaching and the developmental levels of children, being too removed from the front lines—all these conditions work against making the school a personal place where the individuality of the teachers and children provides motivational energy for meaningful learning.

As I consider my new job as a principal, I feel a very strong need to soften and buffer these types of interferences. At last I have the authority and the knowledge to oversee instructional practices, and with the help of the teachers, we will make this a wonderful place for children.

What joy to have the means, finances, personnel, and facilities to ensure that each child will be taught on the correct instructional level. As a principal I can be the instructional leader of this school. I want to be of help in every classroom. Having the total academic picture of the school will help the teachers and me steer the personal instruction of each child every day.

PRIORITIES AND RESOURCES

My highest priority is to help each child leave successful each day. I am totally committed to guiding the instruction of each child—the academic, physical, and emotional development of the child.

Reading and answering mail, maintaining the physical plant, and putting out fires (i.e., discipline problems, parent demands, teacher concerns, keeping the facilities in safe order) can be the major part of a principal's day and easily make up a full-time job. But as the instructional leader, I want to spend the major part of my days in the classrooms, teaching and learning. I begin to consider how I can do this and at the same time be responsible administratively. If my office staff and I can work to free me to get into the classrooms because of a good management style and their commitment, then I know everything can be under control when I am out of the office. This is my challenge.

I plan to set aside at least one hour each day to give my full attention to instruction. My secretary, head custodian, and administrative assistant need to be in on the ground floor about my dreams and expectations. I need their help in recognizing the practicalities of working this out. They are my eyes and ears regarding the climate of the school, and daily contact with them is essential. I want them to feel as important as they truly are to me and to the school.

The teachers' knowledge of the children, the school history, and the parents are great resources for getting to know about each child. My hope is that I will get to know each child and his or her reading level and progress from year to year.

Teachers need to clearly see that they are supported in doing what is truly in the best interest of each child. The goal of doing what is in the best interest of each child may sound simplistic, but there are major obstacles to having the best learning environment in a classroom. One very simple example is the number of interruptions a teacher may have during a typical school day. Interruptions from the intercom for announcements, parents collecting children for appointments, fire drills, other teachers, phone calls from parents, and questions from the office make the list long! These need to be kept to a minimum. For instance, we established that there were to be no announcements over the intercom during the instructional day. We set specific times, at the beginning and end of the day, for announcements.

MY FIRST DAY ON THE JOB

As the new principal at Prescott Elementary School, an older K–5 school that serves 500 children from several neighborhoods, mostly low income, I am eager to get to work. Every principal remembers the first day on the job. A rush of excitement still comes over me as I remember walking onto the campus early on that warm summer morning, the first day of July. The summer staff of three custodians, one secretary, and one clerk greet me enthusiastically, and I am pleased by their enthusiasm. They are friendly and anxious to get to know me. These are critical people in determining a principal's success.

The head custodian, George, takes me through the campus. He tells me about some problems, especially about the overcrowded classrooms, and points with pride to the just-waxed wooden floors in the rooms, the individual cleanliness of each desk, and the beautiful landscaped yards.

Many ideas whirl through my head as I finish a second complete tour of the school alone. Then, on my way back to the office that morning, I make two decisions immediately. I will meet and get together with each member of my instructional staff, the ones who are not away on vacation, within the next three weeks before school officially begins, to learn about past instructional practices at Prescott and to convey to my faculty and staff my determination to make the school a personally satisfying place for each child and each teacher.

Before I unpack my personal belongings in my office, I draft a letter to my teachers and ask them to volunteer one hour to come to the school this summer and meet with me. To get to the core of instruction, the letter contains three questions to be considered before our interview: (1) "Are there any specific materials that I can purchase for you to help you improve instruction in your classroom this year?" (2) "What do you see as the main problem here at Prescott that is detrimental to the learning environment?" and (3) "What is your favorite grade and subject?"

I hope that the letter will prompt teachers to process their answers before we meet. I want them to get a clear message that instruction is my priority. I hope that the individual meetings will show them my eagerness about forming an instructional team and being responsive to their interests.

MEETING MY STAFF AND FACULTY

That first week, my first staff member to come in is my administrative assistant, Betsy. She is a full-time first grade teacher and a part-time administrator. She has lived in the neighborhood for years, knows the families, is respected by the parents, and is a wonderful resource. A few minutes into our first meeting we find ourselves totally in sync about values in education. I am thrilled with her acute understanding of the community.

Right away we eagerly express our views about instruction. The words coming out of her mouth are just like mine. As a first grade teacher, she says that successful reading for each child is her highest priority. Children come first with her at all times. We both have been in the trenches for many years. We believe that a sound discipline policy and consistency are the keys to maintaining a safe and orderly school. We set aside a date to discuss our rules for the entire school. We both realize that we have to set the tone for the teachers and children the minute they come on the campus.

Even though we share the same value system, I can tell immediately that we are very different in the way we approach life. Betsy is very down to earth, a practical realist, who is quiet, unassuming, and careful with her thoughts, language, and details. I know that she will be a great resource to me in understanding the present-day needs of running the school. In contrast, I am more of a whole-picture person, who needs a practical person to keep me grounded in reality!

Just as I will do with each teacher who comes for an interview, I ask her the three questions at our first meeting. I begin: "Are there specific materials I can purchase, before school starts, to help you improve instruction?"

She replies, "I will need the large colored paper rolls to cover my bulletin boards in the classroom. The stand that holds the rolls, in the teacher's lounge, is empty. I like to get attractive displays up in the classrooms so the parents and children will feel excited about the school year when they come into the room!" I make a note. (Good grief! I would never have even thought of this! Thank goodness I asked! All the teachers will need this paper their first day back at school.)

I continue: "What do you see as the main problem here at Prescott that is detrimental to the learning environment?"

Betsy replies: "We have had inadequate discipline (control of children) in some classrooms and a lack of support from the office (principal). Our principal retired last January, and we had an interim principal from the district office for six months. The district person had dual responsibilities. He was principal here but also had his full-time district office job. We did a lot of our own discipline, and some teachers aren't that good at it."

Finally, I ask: "What is your favorite grade and subject?"

Betsy answers: "My favorite grade is first grade, and my favorite subject is reading. I think reading is the most important subject we have to teach."

She continues: "I just want to do the best I can while still teaching first grade. My job is to help you. However, I feel great responsibility for the children I teach. . . . I want all the children in this school to read and love learning. I don't want us to make excuses for any children just because they are poor or don't have a mom and/or dad. . . . I want them all to *be somebody*! Every day when I see children not trying their best because of difficult problems at home, I tell them: 'You are *somebody,* and I love you. But you remember you are *somebody,* and you must work every day to do your best!'"

What a priceless person! I leave the conference with appreciation and enthusiasm to be sharing my job with this excellent educator. Although we met for only an hour, she has already given me confidence that we can make a good team.

GETTING DOWN TO ESSENTIALS

The next day, as I drive into the parking lot, whom do I see but Betsy! She was supposed to leave to go out of town for her vacation yesterday. I wonder why she did not leave. But as I ask her why she is back today, she says, "I just felt like I'd better come in today and help you go over what needs to be done before the teachers and children get here." I say, giving her a *big* hug, "You are such a blessing!"

She shows me boxes of new textbooks that need to be inventoried and marked with the Prescott stamp and supplies for each class that are not yet checked in by the invoice (crayons, construction paper, writing paper, etc.). Then she gives me a list of all the children's names in the school. They need to be assigned to classrooms. Also, she tells me that all the furniture in the school has to be counted and reported to the district office.

In addition to these duties, I also need to order additional custodial supplies for the entire school—supplies that are needed in the office, clinic, and classrooms; in the art, music, and physical education departments; and by the custodial staff. These supplies include such items as bathroom tissue, office supplies, paper towels, and so forth. The supply budget for a school of our size is about $40,000. This excludes instructional materials, such as books, workbooks, charts, posters, and instructional printed materials.

As we study our enrollment, per grade, and find that the class size ranges between twenty-seven and thirty-five students, we know that we have a problem: not enough children's desks. The county projection for our school was twenty-five to twenty-nine students per classroom. Betsy and I go over the lists again, and we match children registered with the desks in each classroom. George, my head custodian, goes to the warehouse and gets old discarded desks that are free. He will repair and refinish them before school starts—we hope. Because of George we will have a desk for each child with minimal added expense. George is another great blessing—another terrific worker and wonderful resource! All these activities are what I call necessary essentials. They draw me away from what I would rather be doing: reading the students' cumulative folders and interviewing the teachers.

Getting the classrooms stocked, cleaned, and ready is an arduous task for us all. But the humming of lawnmowers, the shouting of greetings from children in the neighborhood, the ringing of the telephone, and the many, many jobs to do are exciting. The campus is full of anticipation and joy for the first day of school. Teachers drop by to meet me, children poke their heads in the classrooms as we uncrate books, parents call with questions, and delivery trucks keep bringing needed supplies and books. The campus is humming away, and I am totally "in the zone" of loving life and my job!

PRESCOTT ELEMENTARY

A little bit about the school: Prescott Elementary houses about 500 students who attend kindergarten through the fifth grade. The school is located in a low-income neighborhood. The student population is 60 percent poverty level or below, 20 percent lower middle income, 10 percent middle income, and 10 percent high income. Drug-bust raids and police surveillance are not uncommon in the neighborhood immediately surrounding the school.

Built in 1958, Prescott is a red brick school with separate classroom wings. Each wing houses one or two different grade levels. The art, music, and physical education facilities are in a separate wing, and the media center is in a building of its own. The landscaped yards, the trimmed shrubbery, and the neatly cut grass are a tribute to the skill of the head custodian. In addition, there are two large fields for physical education, one with a small hard-topped space.

The teachers at Prescott have an average teaching experience of twenty-one years. The average age is fifty. A majority of the teachers began their career here and have never taught anywhere else. This is also essentially true for the noninstructional staff.

ROACH INFESTATION!

That first week, before I meet with any of the faculty, George and I go around to every classroom to put a final approval on each room's cleanliness and readiness. When I start my inspection, I am curious about the large paneled closets in the back of each room. Each closet contains the teacher's personal supplies and equipment. They are locked for the summer. Above each closet is a small unlocked overhead cupboard.

Climbing up on a small ladder, I begin to look in these cupboards and, in some classrooms, discover old student papers and stacks of old newspapers. I look at the dates of the newspapers and discover some from 1962! For decades these papers have been in these cupboards. I ask George to bring me huge trash barrels, and we begin cleaning out the cupboards. We start to find roach eggs and droppings. I decide to notify the maintenance department and have it send someone out to look in the attic of the school. This is a disturbing discovery!

The next day the maintenance supervisor comes into my office looking somewhat drained and a little pale. He sits down heavily on the chair across from me and says: "We do have a bit of a problem here. You have *literally tons* of roaches. So many, in fact, that they are inches deep in the attic. The live ones are feeding on the carcasses of other dead roaches and the papers. Roaches love the glue on the newspapers. They have evidently been up there for years."

I hate roaches! I try to be as professional as possible: "*Oh, my God, what can we do?* If we spray them, they will come crawling out all over the place. Have my teachers been so negligent about throwing out and cleaning?"

"Well ma'am," he replies, "when you have tons of paper and an old school, this is not so uncommon. However, I have to tell you, this is the worst I've seen. It's our problem, not yours. We will fumigate on a weekend and come back and clean up."

What an awesome task! I remind myself to give him a call on Friday and tell him that I will leave sodas, coffee, and some donuts for them in the teacher's lounge. I certainly want to establish good relationships with all the district maintenance people.

Second, I immediately start looking, fearfully, about my office. I go into the storage closet and see boxes and boxes of storage. I wonder if I have the same problem in my office space!

The next day I wear shorts and an old T-shirt, crawl up on a ladder, and start to work in the storage closet, which has been housing old records for years. I begin throwing away old records—some, I found out later, that I was supposed to keep, but I did not get into trouble about this. I am in a frenzy of cleanliness to overcome this horror. Sure enough, I see the ugly evidence as I pull away old boxes.

After a few hours at work, I am dirty, dusty, and, by this time, in my bare feet. From the front office only about five feet away, I hear my secretary say, "May I help you, sir?"

"Yes, you may. I am here to see Dr. Lawrence." I hear my secretary reply, "I'm sorry, sir, she is very busy today. She does not have anyone down for an appointment this afternoon. I'm afraid she isn't expecting anyone."

This secretary is new on the job and one of 5,000 school district employees. She does not recognize the school superintendent. But I recognize his voice immediately. I am standing helplessly, barefoot, *trapped* in the closet outside my office.

Dr. Smith replies, "I'm Dr. Jim Smith, the school superintendent, and would really like to see her if she is here. May I just go on in?" The school secretary rather helplessly says, "She is in the closet to your right, sir." I am inside the closet, filthy, and standing on a small ladder. I am just appalled that this is my first encounter with Dr. Smith since he hired me.

With as much dignity as I can muster, I crawl down from the ladder in front of the superintendent, put on my shoes, and ask him to come into my office. As I try to get him comfortable, I wonder if he will notice how dirty I am. Talking about how much I am enjoying my new job, I casually go over to the sink in my office and begin to wash my hands while noting, with dismay, the dirt and dust all over my arms and legs.

I can tell that he is curious about what I have been doing, but he waits until I am seated and asks, "Well, how has everything been going for you?"

"Fine," I somewhat calmly reply with a little hysteria in my voice. "Everything is just fine. Today I just happen to have a little roach problem." Somewhat perplexed, he says, "How does a principal have a little roach problem?" Finally, I just say to myself, "Oh, what the heck!" I tell him the whole story.

He laughs at my discomfort and tells me that he is impressed that I have such a positive attitude about it. He applauds me for "getting in the thick of things," and we both laugh. I can tell that he is a wonderful man with a good sense of humor. I only remember my mortification and his kindness to me. I am so thankful that he is pleased instead of thinking that this might not be in my job description.

This visit proves to be one of several conversations with a new superintendent who is very much a visionary. After we talked, I knew I was supported in my plans for instruction.

AN INTERVIEW ABOUT F GRADES

The next week I begin to learn about past instructional practices at the school. I put aside one hour each day to gather data from written records in each child's cumulative folder. I promised myself I would read all of them. A child's cumulative folder follows the child from kindergarten through the twelfth grade. The folders give great information about scores on nationally normed tests, teacher comments from year to year, health records, notes from parents, and other significant data. I can check aptitude scores and see if the child's achievement is commensurate with the scores. The teacher's personal written comments shed much light on the attitude of the teacher, the behavior and ability of the child, and the student's year-to-year progress.

As I read the entries and inserts in the folders, from kindergarten to the present year, I can tell a lot about how a child has progressed. The summary comment required for each child by the teacher at the end of the year gives me insight also about the teacher's view of children.

While looking through a fourth grade teacher's folders, I discover that the teacher, Jane, gave twenty failures (Fs) in science last year, in a class of thirty-three children. The children in previous years had a normal spread of grades in science—some average, some below, and some high. A red flag registers in my brain. Why so many failures? I make a note to ask the teacher about this perplexity.

When I see two-thirds of a class getting Fs in science, I suspect that there is a problem in the instruction. My value system and past teaching experience tell me that if a teacher has more than a few failures in any subject, the material is not being taught properly or the reading level is too high.

I make a call. "Jane, this is Carolyn Lawrence. I apologize for calling you during vacation. I'm trying to meet as many of our teachers on the staff as possible this summer. Would you consider coming in to visit with me at your convenience?"

Jane comes in the next afternoon. She is a very attractive, tall, thin woman who has taught at the school for about fifteen years. She has always received high evaluations on her teaching ability but average and below-average ones on her public relations skills.

"Thanks for coming in. I'm Dr. Lawrence, and I am excited about being here. I want us to work as closely as possible for the best education for your children. Are there specific materials I can purchase, before school starts, to help you improve instruction?"

"Well, we do need four new microscopes for the science department storeroom."

"I'm sure our budget can handle that order. If you will just give me the particular model and kind that you want, I'll try to have them in here as soon as possible. What do you see as the main problem here at Prescott that is detrimental to the learning environment?"

Jane replies, "There doesn't seem to be enough coordination about instruction between the grade levels. I would like to have more time for interaction with the primary teachers."

Gratefully, I thank her for that suggestion and tell her that we will try to have interaction between grade levels, not just at the end of the year but during the year as well. Then I ask, "What is your favorite grade and subject?"

"I definitely would like to stay at the fourth grade level. I taught kindergarten for several years, then fourth grade. I like fourth grade much better. I especially enjoy teaching science. Because of my love for science, I usually am the coordinator for science for the school."

As we look over the assignment for grade levels, I am pondering just the right way to approach Jane about the percentage of science failures in her class. She is very straightforward, and I am thankful for that. She is comfortable with what she wants to do. That is great, too. She is a strong, confident teacher. I love that about her.

"My goal is to give every teacher the best placement I can—to match the children's needs. I am very pleased that you know exactly what you want and are excited about fourth grade. I certainly don't see any problem right now with you staying with fourth grade. But I haven't met with all the teachers. My policy, however, is that I will not change a teacher's grade from last year unless absolutely necessary." I smile reassuringly.

"There is one particular concern I have about science in fourth grade, however, that I need to ask you about. When looking through all the students' cumulative folders, I noticed that in fourth grade you had 35 percent of your children fail science last year. Would you mind telling me about your view of science instruction here at Prescott and the criteria you used to determine grades?"

She nods at me enthusiastically. "Yes, I'll be more than happy to explain. I am very concerned about the background in science the children are getting here. The children come to me from third grade with almost *no knowledge* of the basic fundamentals in science. I think it is my duty to teach them fourth grade science. I can't pass the children, however, on fourth grade level in science when they don't even know what the concepts mean! Their former teachers need to get the children better prepared for science before they come to fourth grade. I teach *fourth* grade science, not first, second, or third grade in science.

"Let me explain. I start at the beginning of the science book, and we have an outline from the district staff that tells us how much we are to cover each six weeks. I *have* to cover this material because it is on the fourth grade achievement test at the end of the year. Most of my children just don't care about science, and many times I have to fail these children to get the parents' and the child's *attention!*"

I feel the hair rise on the back of my neck. I want to *quickly* reply, *"You are hired to teach children at whatever level they come to you, in any subject!"* In my previous years as instructional leader of three schools, I heard this same rationale *many* times. The greatest obstacle to connecting with children on their own particular instructional level is the district curriculum and instructional plans. These overall plans are governed by national tests. This district's staff has outlined each grade level, tells the teachers *exactly* what they are to teach and when they are to teach it, and many times gives suggestions on how the material is to be taught. The district does this to get students ready for national *tests* because it is under so much public pressure about tests scores, entrance exams for college, and accountability.

As I write these pages years later, teachers are feeling pressure "to cover material" even more now than when I was a principal. Teachers who are former colleagues tell me that they must document when and how everything has been covered in their lesson plans regardless of the levels of their children, or their school may be labeled an F school! Our curriculum and teachers are being driven by grade level and national achievement tests, regardless of the instructional level of each child.

To Jane I say, "I certainly do understand where you are coming from. With all you have to teach, you certainly want children to be at a particular science level when you start working with them. I do promise you that I will see that the primary teachers work on this.

"However, even in fourth grade science, you must determine what prerequisite concepts and skills the children have *not* obtained in science and teach them these foundation skills. Even if your children need first or second grade science concepts, these are the skills they must be taught. This means, at first, that they may not be ready for the fourth grade test. I can live with that, and I will be responsible for dealing with the media and district staff if we have ramifications. I have already talked with the area superintendent about allowing our school not to be driven by tests. Rather, we have a more feasible long-range plan to concentrate on helping the individual child. This will be hard at first, but you and I can monitor what is happening in science throughout the school, and we will make good progress.

"I would very much like for you to be my science contact person for the school, if you would. By having you as the science contact, we will determine exactly which skills are missing when they get to fourth grade." (This means that Jane will be the spokesperson for new science information coming from the district to the faculty, will be in charge of the science fair [competition among schools], and will make suggestions for the improvement of science instruction.) Jane smiles and quickly agrees to have this job again.

"Let's come back to your twenty children who failed science. I checked their cumulative folders and found that many of them did not have a fourth grade reading level. Is it possible they did poorly with the science concepts because they couldn't read and understand the textbook? Having all children on a particular level at one time is rarely possible in any subject. But as I'm sure you know, science is a subject that can be taught with less dependence on reading than some other subjects. I know you use experiments, cooperative learning activities, and hands-on-type experiences where they can learn with concrete action.

"With the instruction centered on activities, the textbook is used mostly as a resource, and skill and concept acquisition is less dependent on reading. This is one way to deal with so many different reading levels. Otherwise, I believe we make a mistake in giving assignments to those students who cannot read at grade level, and that only diminishes their interest in science. . . . Our job is to bring the children as far along in science as we can. I can help you with more supplies for experiments or whatever you think you need."

Jane replies: "Dr. Lawrence, I appreciate what you are trying to do. But I just disagree with you. If we don't have certain expectations for children at a certain level, then how can we *ever* expect our society to get better? I have made lists of concepts for the primary teachers of what should be taught before the children get to my classroom. The primary teachers just haven't responded. I have even talked with *each* primary teacher about my concerns, and they don't seem to care! We are talking about getting children to learn some science concepts before they get to fourth grade—we need more help in this area."

"Jane, I really want to work with you on this, and I agree wholeheartedly that I need to check to see that foundation concepts are being taught in the primary grades. But I have a few reasons for my concern with the number of failures in any subject in the elementary school.

"The first reason is the effect on self-esteem of the students. We have a multitude of research to show that *children's ability to achieve is 75 percent related to their self-esteem as learners when they come into contact with new material.* If they are continually defeated, they quit trying. So that they can perceive themselves as able learners, our children need to have successes every day. And the successes come only as instruction is matched to their conceptual and skills levels. It is possible.

"Jane, try not to let this conversation get you down. I am *not* trying to run your classroom. Just reflect about what we have talked about. When school starts we will put our minds together and, with input from the faculty, come up with help from the primary teachers on teaching more basic science concepts, and I will adjust the budget to get you more resources for experiments and hands-on learning if you need them."

Jane replies, "Well, if you can really help me, this will be the first time I have *ever* received instructional support from a principal. Usually the principal doesn't even know what we are going through. I welcome the ideas, but I think you are idealistic and not putting enough responsibility on the students!"

"Perhaps that's true. I do appreciate your honesty with me and your candor. And don't worry, I will not accept students not doing their part. I can see how much you care about children and their learning. This is *by far* the most important aspect, in my estimation, of a good teacher. We will work out the rest."

AN ASIDE ABOUT SCHOOL FINANCING

As Jane stands to go, I stand and shake her hand. I try to give her a calm message from my heart and not let her see how distressed I am. Dear God, I think, when can we ever ensure that all children have equal opportunity in our public school system? By having so many children in a classroom and by letting the curriculum be driven by tests, we are failing many of our children who are already at risk.

Florida, at this time, ranks twenty-sixth in median family income compared with the other forty-nine states. Yet we rank forty-seventh in per-pupil spending for education, partly because we have no state income tax. Silently I rage at the inadequate funding for education that causes the crowding of classrooms. With so little time for individual attention, this makes teaching that much harder. I know the research shows that eighteen is the maximum number of students for optimal learning in a primary classroom. Why am I looking at thirty-five children in each of our fourth grade classrooms at Prescott?

At Prescott I also know that we have the added burden of no air-conditioning in our school, the same as many of the older schools in our district. Because of the hot days of spring and fall, the effective hours of instruction are cut considerably. Also, the budget limits us to six-hour school days. Transporting children is expensive and requires many school buses. Each school bus costs between $80,000 and $120,000. To save money, each bus makes a high school, middle school, and then elementary school run each morning and each afternoon.

Many teachers and parents *want* a longer school day. Money is the problem. Tax moneys are not squandered in our schools. In all my thirty-two years in education, working in seven different districts and three states, I have yet to see a district with too many administrators, salaries that are too high, or any misuse of funds. I have not encountered many rich superintendents, principals, or teachers or very many classrooms that are equipped with all they need to instruct properly!

INTERVIEW WITH A CARING SECOND GRADE TEACHER

After my conversation with Jane, I make a note to myself about the problem of basic science concepts being taught in the primary grades and tell my secretary that I am ready for my next interview. She is a second grade teacher who has been at Prescott all her career. Dorothy Blalock has taught second grade for twenty-seven years. When reading her remarks in her children's cumulative folders from the previous year, I found that she is very caring, does not use negative language, and has many statements that lead me to believe that she cares and understands much about correct instructional level.

Her comments reflect that she is very intelligent and also sees something positive about each child.

As she enters, I actually feel her positive energy and concern. She is very soft spoken and leads into the conversation with, "Dr. Lawrence, I am so grateful to have this opportunity to meet with you before school starts. I have heard good things about you, and I feel that we share much of the same ideas about children."

"Well, Mrs. Blalock, I have had only good comments about your tenure and you at Prescott. I see that your teacher evaluations have been outstanding. As the new school year starts, how can I help you?"

"Dr. Lawrence, reading is my favorite subject, and in that context I would like to address the first question you sent to me in your letter. You asked about what we need before we start school, to improve instruction. I need books—short books with few pages—for the children to practice reading at home. Because we don't send the instructional reading texts home, most of the children need other books that are on their reading level. They need different stories with the same small instructional vocabulary. Can you think of how we can get something for them to read at home? The books will need to be kindergarten, first, and second grade levels, with a few books on third grade too."

I reply, "Yes, I think we have a source. I will check. The district warehouse stores old reading texts that are outdated. One of the best parts about these old books is that they are recycled to the schools for free. I used some of them last year, and we can actually give them to the children to keep as their own! With any luck, according to how many are there, we may be able to find all the levels you need. This way we can start building the number of books in the home.

"In addition to these books, there is another very good program for new books for children. You may have heard of it. It is called Reading Is Fundamental, RIF for short. It is a government program funded to help all children get more books into their homes. We obtain the books by writing a grant and explaining why we need the books. The government will give us an amount of money for the books, with the stipulation that we match the funds from our Parent Teacher Association [PTA]. They must pay half of the price of each book. We can make this a project for this year! Our school advisory council meets with the PTA next week. We will see if we can raise the funds, if they approve the project. The classroom teacher gets to decide which books and what levels are best for the children in a class."

Mrs. Blalock says, "Wow, that sounds great! I'll be willing to help write the grant, Dr. Lawrence, and you'll take this to the school advisory committee and check on the books at the warehouse. You just give me the forms for the grant, and I will work with the other teachers about getting these extra books from the RIF program!"

When I have a good teacher, as Mrs. Blalock seems to be, my plan is to funnel all kinds of materials and supplies to support her. Just as children learn from each other in a wonderful manner, teachers who trust each other often love to help and learn from each other. I will use her as a peer teacher when I hire beginning teachers in the future. This type of peer assistance is so much more effective than assistance coming from outside of the classroom.

I continue, "Reading books at home at night can be integrated with my new homework policy. I require every child to have at least twenty minutes of homework each night in the primary grades. If you have the children read one of their on-level books to a parent at night, this could help with your assignments. Homework must be assigned and then checked in the mornings when the children come to school. One day a week you might assign reading as the homework and have them bring in a note from a parent. When I taught first and second grades, I always used the supplementary reading sheets that went with each reading group for their homework or sometimes their morning seat work to be corrected. But I can see that you could just get a note from the parents saying the child read for twenty minutes with one of your books."

"That's a great idea. I have always given homework myself to build up that kind of expectation about school in each child. I am so glad to hear that you will make that requirement schoolwide. Will the upper grades have homework too?"

"Yes," I reply, "but it will not be limited to twenty minutes. But all homework in every grade will have to be checked in each morning, and the child will have to be given credit for doing it. But if the teachers agree, I like the children to have free weekends unless they have a long-term project they are working on completing."

I then ask, "Mrs. Blalock, what do you see happening at Prescott that is detrimental to instruction?"

"The dividing of children into different subject areas during the day and changing teachers. I really like to have my children all day and hate to teach many different children during a day. Do you think we could go back to self-contained classrooms? I really believe, in my experience, they are better for the children, and I know they are better for me, personally."

I reply: "Mrs. Blalock, I am working on this issue, and we have to weigh a lot of factors. I agree with you about this being the most effective teaching method, but I haven't gotten far enough along, at this point, to see if I can bring it about."

"I understand, Dr. Lawrence, and I will support either way, but I love teaching all subjects in second grade. So much of sound education involves incorporating one subject into another one and not separating reading from language arts or math from science. When I can extend one set of skills through another subject, then the knowledge base is so much more solid, and I really feel I am teaching to mastery."

I can see that we have much in common, and I know we could go on talking all day, with our similar interests and views about instruction, but my next teacher is waiting. I thank her warmly for being so open with me about her views of instruction and her commitment to the children. I express my delight that she likes self-contained classrooms, and I promise to support her in every way that I can. I also promise that she can have second grade, if at all possible.

MEETING WITH THE FORMER PRINCIPAL

So as I meet with other teachers I gather more data about past instructional practices. I become aware that the children are not grouped heterogeneously for instruction. The children are homogeneously (ability) grouped by subject. In other words, the children change classrooms and teachers several times a day. This is a form of departmentalization and is more often used in middle and high schools.

To glean further information, I decide to call the former principal of this school and ask him about departmentalization, specifically, and any other information he wants to share. He very kindly agrees to go to lunch with me. He is a *very* cordial man. We have known each other for some while, beginning when I was an assistant principal for instruction in another school in the district. He is a wonderful, practical, down-to-earth educator who was well loved by his staff at Prescott. Our first conversation begins like this: "I am so excited about Prescott! The campus is beautiful. You've done a great job of maintaining a plant built in 1958. The teachers speak of having a wonderful rapport with you. I want to keep it that way but need tips on how you did these good things and still had time to work on other problems."

Mr. Dunning is a tall, distinguished man of about sixty who always seems to have a smile lurking in his eyes. He has a tremendous sense of humor and an overall good nature and is known for speaking his mind and being well respected by his peers. I know he lived through hard times at this school. He does not seem to be as enthusiastic about my possibilities for making great strides in helping the teachers.

He begins with a suggestion: "Let's start by discussing the plant attractiveness. George, your head custodian, is a big plus for you in keeping your campus clean and beautiful. He is one of the best in the district. I hired him right out of high school, and after five years, he has proven to be great! Depend on him to look after the outside of the plant and the classrooms."

"Yes! I can do that," I say to myself. Looking after the physical plant of the school is just not my forte, to say the least. George will be a great help!

Again, Mr. Dunning's smile lurks behind his eyes. "Just show him appreciation and *listen* to his advice. Remember, he doesn't like cleaning individual classrooms but loves to keep the outside looking beautiful. Let him run the custodian staff as he sees fit. Then you can't go wrong."

I have already told George that we will go to lunch, alone, about twice a month. I know that my head custodian and secretary will be great assets. Head custodians and school secretaries know more about the inner workings of the school than any other people. They are tremendously important to the success of a school.

I tell Mr. Dunning about my next concern, which is my preference for heterogeneous grouping. "While studying research on best instructional practices, I find it hard to support the practice of children changing classes and teachers so often during the day! I cannot imagine primary grade children working well without being able to bond with a particular teacher all day long. The little children, especially, need the security. Changing classrooms several times each day means each child loses many precious instructional minutes daily."

I knew as a former first and second grade teacher that I needed to be with my children all day long. I continue, "When children first encounter the reading process, the teacher *must* spend a *lot* of time encouraging the process. Constant reinforcement is essential throughout the day as the slow readers encounter hard words in other subjects."

This would not be the first time Mr. Dunning brought me back to reality: "I know your research is probably correct. But Prescott has a few very poor teachers. I chose not to leave children with a poor or marginal teacher all day long. I rotated the children through good, marginal, and poor teachers during the day so that no child was subject to bad teaching all day long."

My heart sinks a little, but I believe that my experience with recognizing problems in instruction and dealing with them might make it possible to go with heterogeneous grouping. Not surprisingly, marginal teachers, on tenure for life, are sometimes transferred from a more affluent school into a school with more poverty populations. Parents who are poor have less time to worry about how a teacher is doing with their children! Trying to survive daily with essential food, clothing, and housing occupies most of their time. For whatever reasons, their expectations of teachers are likely to be substantially lower than those of more affluent parents. Also, well-qualified new teachers tend to be attracted to, and sought out by, schools serving more affluent families.

In Florida, as with other states in the country, there is a very specific plan for the dismissal of incompetent teachers on tenure. This involves much documentation and assistance to the teacher, but even tenured teachers can lose their license for poor performance if the arduous process is followed to the end. As I end my conversation with Mr. Dunning, I have a suspicion that I may have to pursue the dismissal plan with one or more teachers. Each dismissal for a tenured teacher takes from one to three years.

INTERVIEW WITH THE MEDIA CENTER SPECIALIST

I return to school after lunch for my next conference. It is with the media specialist, who is waiting in my office. She is a seasoned veteran of thirty-one years at this school. I had been advised by the district media director that Mrs. Chance is a formidable woman, a leader in the community, and an officer in the district's teachers' union. The media director told me that Mrs.

Chance's outdated media methods are long-standing and that she isolates herself in the media center. I will try very hard to be accommodating, professional, and sincere. I am eager for a kindred spirit in the media center. It is, to me, the single most important area in any school. Because of my enthusiasm for the media center, I *strongly* believe that I will win her over completely within this thirty-minute period.

"Mrs. Chance, thanks for meeting with me. I'd like to hear some of your needs and expectations about running the media center. I've just recently come from a school where the media center was a dynamic place constantly filled with children and teachers!"

Mrs. Chance replies, somewhat defensively, "I am very upset about the new district program of open scheduling." (This means that children and teachers are free to go into the media center at any time, without prior notification, to secure materials, do research, etc.) "I need children to come to the media only at their allotted times. My other *major* problem is my display case in the media. It is locked, and I haven't been able to get into it for three years. I want to open the case to get the old sports trophies out and replace them!"

I can tell we definitely have different priorities! *Good grief,* three years with a locked display case? I cannot believe it. *These are her two biggest priorities? (Really!* Give me a break!) Tread carefully, Carolyn, I caution myself; You don't want to alienate this teacher in the first five minutes.

I very quickly reply, "Certainly we can work on the display case! I'll get that done today! About open scheduling—I have to admit I am very much for the concept. I feel the media center is the 'hub' of the school. I think it's essential that it be open at all times to the children. But we will need to work on it in a gradual way. In order to move that way, you will definitely need to have additional help."

She draws a *very* resolute deep breath, rising to her most forbidding self in her chair, and glares at me. She says, "I teach study skills to *every* third grader—every year. I am responsible for checking out books and materials and ordering new materials. I cannot and will not have children running in and out of the media at any time. I need all media center times to be scheduled. I work times into *my* schedule with the teacher."

Oh, boy, this teacher is scary. For now, I had better not have a confrontation, but I will not give up on my commitment to open scheduling. "Judy, I certainly do understand what you are saying. I know media specialists are overworked. I'll support you, always. I will, however, want to work on open scheduling this year. We can work it out. I may even have to give you some of my office staff's hours each day, so you won't be interrupted while you are teaching study skills."

"Dr. Lawrence, I *started* this media center thirty-one years ago in a regular classroom! I have an incredibly busy schedule and good communication with the teachers, but I will not have children come in and out of the center all the time. I have too many responsibilities to allow this to happen."

Calmly I reply, "I *do* understand what you are saying, and I know open scheduling must seem like a radical concept. However, children need to come for research or books when they are motivated and enthusiastic. I know you have heard of the *'teachable moment'*? You are *my most* vital teacher in the school because you can inspire the love of *reading*! Nothing is more important to me. By your union contract, you have a duty-free lunch, two fifteen-minute breaks, and a thirty-minute planning period each day. My primary responsibility, and I know you can understand, is to provide the best instruction I can for each child. As the instructional leader, I have to decide, with you, how we can do this most effectively. A media center is a resource center, an enticing, pulsating place where children and teachers love to come and explore! Together we can make this a reality for Prescott!"

She is very shut down. "I am just one person. I'm required to teach reference skills to all third graders, and I read a story to each classroom every other week to emphasize different types of literature. Additionally, every teacher is scheduled to bring her whole class and check out books every other week. I refresh fifth graders' media skills three weeks before their achievement test. I do so many other jobs, I don't see how I can have children just coming and going all the time."

Realizing I am fighting a losing battle, I calm myself and put away my need to grab and shake her! I listen to Mrs. Chance quietly. I realize that she cannot conceptualize this change and is fearful. I feel sorry for her and make a mental note to reschedule another conference and try to bring her along. I also need input from the rest of the faculty about the effectiveness of the media center. We depart from the conference with my promise to call a locksmith. She is somewhat mollified but still leaves very displeased and unsettled.

After several conferences with teachers, I begin to notice a tendency of some teachers to tell me about negative aspects of the school and the staff. Many teachers and staff feel that by blaming others in the past they will ingratiate themselves with me. I am quick to tell them, professionally and ethically, that I am not interested in any past unpleasantness. This is very important. There is no way, with the vastness of the responsibilities of the principalship, that I could possibly second-guess the decisions made before I arrived. I am determined to always make a positive statement, such as "I have heard so many good things about this school," and go right on with the conversation. I notice after several such statements that my staff seems to begin to get the message.

Following many conversations with teachers, parents, and staff, I get busy planning for the start of school. I have to get each of my teachers assigned to a particular grade and classroom. Every year principals in the district are given, during the summer, an allotment of teachers for the next year. This is based on the projected number of students coming to the school for the following year. Most of the time, the total estimation of students is very close to the number that shows up the first day of school. It is less accurate about the numbers in any particular grade. Often, teachers have to be shifted to another grade level to accommodate a particularly large group moving from one grade to the next.

After interviewing all the teachers, I begin to get a picture of how wedded each teacher is to a particular grade. Knowing this is helpful when I have to make room designations and grade assignments. As a former teacher and assistant principal for instruction, I know that most teachers do better in the grade of their choice. Some teachers are great in any grade. Some teachers have been in a certain grade too long and are getting stale and negative. Meeting with the teachers and listening carefully to them provided me with much valuable data. My overall impression is that I am lucky to have such good people, and I feel much needed and respected by all.

3

DISCIPLINE

The first day of school is tomorrow, and what a job we have had getting everything ready! Every day brought a variety of problems and complex situations. The most unexpected and time-consuming task has entailed dealing with parents who demand to choose the teacher for their child. Every parent wants the "best" teacher for his or her child. The teachers have been at Prescott for many years and naturally have earned specific reputations. In daily parent conferences, the parents told me their particular reasons why their child should be given special consideration.

To get all children assigned within a plan of heterogeneous grouping (one high-level, one average, and one low-level reading group in each classroom), children have to be placed without regard to requests. My rule with all parents is that the parents must let me place the children. After three weeks, if the child is emotionally or physically unable to stay with a certain teacher, the child could be reassigned. I knew from past experience that after a child has settled into the routine of the teacher, the requests to change classes will be very few. But I was sincere when I told the parents that I would not leave a child in a class if there were a real problem.

There were approximately fifty of these types of conversation with parents within the six weeks before school started. After the first five or six conferences, I realized that my absolute refusal to waver was essential for the assignment plan of getting the children placed, and it helped to retain my sanity. Because of past practices at this school, I realized, I walked a very thin line between alienating the parents and gaining their support. This was difficult and scary. Thank goodness I was aware of the research that has found leaders (school principals) most effective when they make decisions and stick by them—even if the decisions prove to be wrong at a later date.

OUR FIRST DAY OF SCHOOL

Around 9:30 AM on opening day, all the adults in the school breathe a sign of relief! All 487 children are settled in their classrooms. I call the district office to report on our numbers in each class. I am thrilled that our collective organizing and planning have worked. Especially important was the "Greet the Teacher Day" we had last week for children to meet their teachers and find their classrooms before the first day of school.

As I suspected, all the classrooms are overcrowded. To my mind we have pulled off a magnificent feat by putting each child in a class. Calm prevails on the campus. I feel a tremendous urge to show my appreciation to every staff member for being so cooperative and helpful. I also have a need to meet the children and check to see that all is well. As I leave the office, I tell the staff that I am going to visit each classroom and introduce myself.

As I enter and visit each classroom, I tell each teacher that I appreciate her hard work and help and praise the children for their good conduct. All the first and second grade teachers and children are doing well. They appear receptive, orderly, and on task. When I turn the corner and head for the second wing, I notice that the media center is deserted. Again, I remind myself to work with the media specialist. I will expect activity there soon.

The children and teachers in the second wing are also receptive and orderly. As I introduce myself, I am impressed by the attention and respect shown me. After visiting about twenty classrooms (for roughly five minutes each), I finally approach the last wing. Faintly, I hear a low rumble at the end of the hall. But, lest I forget a class, I faithfully stick to my sequential order and continue to give my pep talk in each classroom. Before I enter the last classroom on the wing, a paper airplane comes sailing through the air and lands at my feet.

Looking across the room, I see a boy climbing out of a *window* on the opposite side of the room and Mrs. Chamblee, a veteran teacher, sobbing at her desk. I rush around the outside of the classroom, grab the child by the arm, and march him right back to the classroom to his empty desk. With *severe* disapproval on my face and indignation in every fiber of my being, I let my voice tremble on the verge of (pretended) rage and with real authority say: "What in the world do you children think you are doing on the *first* day of school? The *oldest* children in this school are supposed to be the *role* models! Here I thought I could count on you to earn a lot of *special* privileges because you are *fifth* graders, our patrols, and our *leaders*! And what do I find but students acting like *kindergartners or first graders.* I am just completely surprised. I guess I may just have to rethink all of our planning about our wonderful year for our fifth graders!"

I ring the office and send for my veteran but just rehired curriculum resource teacher to come to the classroom. I scan the faces of the children quickly. I can tell that the children are feeling relief about the control restored to the class.

"Put your heads down on your desks, close your eyes, and think about what happened today. I want to know everything and will talk with you about it. What do you need to do *today* to be a responsible fifth grader? I know all of you haven't made bad choices about your behavior, but this is *very* serious. I don't want to see one head up while I talk with Mrs. Chamblee."

Grimly, I think to myself, this teacher has been at this school for twenty-nine years! This cannot have been happening all this time. What is going on? How come she cannot control the children on the *first* day when the students are known to be the most orderly and quiet?

Mrs. Ann Greatsy comes into the class from the office with a book under her arm to read to the children. I knew it! She is so dependable and competent and, without my telling her, knows how to help! I silently say, "Thank you, God." Then I usher Mrs. Chamblee to my office and get her a cold drink, and we settle down to talk.

"Mrs. Chamblee, what's happening?"

"Dr. Lawrence, I am so sorry. I just am overtired from working this summer and getting ready for school. The prospect of having another year with at least thirty-four children just got the best of me. I know I can get all this under control, if you will just give me a few minutes."

"You take all the time you need. I know you are a good teacher. You are just having an incredibly bad day, and you *must* pull yourself together. Go back into the room as soon as you feel up to it. I'll go speak with Mrs. Greatsy and ask her to stay."

I rush down the hall to the room, thanking the cosmos for Mrs. Greatsy. Mrs. G. is quietly reading a book to the children, and all is well. Giving her a smile of encouragement I tell her that Mrs. Chamblee will be right back. Then I rush back to the office, and, thankfully, Mrs. Chamblee has gotten herself under control. She is ready to go back and finish the day. This one incident brings home to me, once again, how important it is to visit the classrooms as often as possible.

When I return to the office I have two parents waiting to have a conference with me. My secretary introduces me to Dr. and Mrs. Van Astor and their child. I remember that a school board member called me about Sylvester. He is seven years old and has never been in public school; he has only been to a private church school.

"We're here because we've heard good things about you. Sylvester has been in private school until now because he is gifted, very sensitive, and a special Christian. You know we have to protect him from certain types of children that may damage his innocent way of looking at the world!" (Oh, please, I say to myself. *Give me a break!* I just cannot believe such blatant prejudice! Carolyn, I warn myself, remember, try not to make snap judgments.)

"First," Mrs. Van Astor continues, "we don't want him to get bored. You can count on him to be a model child. He always tells us if he does something wrong. He is our only child and very responsible. We just came to be *sure* he gets the best teacher!"

Smiling at Sylvester and both parents, I say, "Well, he is just the kind of great boy we need in our school, and we are so pleased you trust us with him!"

"Yes, we do trust you," Mrs. Van Astor says, "and we want Mrs. Green to be Sylvester's teacher. We hear she is the *best* teacher in first grade. I am working near here at the university. Dr. Phillips, the chairman of the school board, is a good friend of mine. He assured me you would personally see that

Sylvester gets Mrs. Green." (This is yet another parent pressuring me for a particular teacher—special pressure, using the name of a school board member.)

"Well, I don't take parent requests but can assure you Sylvester will get the best education we can give him. Having the advantage of being a former first grade teacher myself, I can monitor what is happening in each classroom. I think the first grade is the most important year for a child in elementary school. My responsibility is to the children, so you can rest assured he will be treated well. His teacher will be alerted to the fact that this is his first year in public school classrooms, and we will help Sylvester make the adjustment.

"Three weeks from now you can schedule an appointment and give me specifics if you aren't pleased with his teacher. I know you realize with almost 500 children to be placed in classes, we couldn't get school started if I took parents' requests." I am very proud of myself for staying calm and not being intimidated by their use of pressure.

Shocked, the mother replies, *"But we heard you would give Sylvester special attention and take our request.* The only reason we are contemplating moving him here is because we have been told you are so caring about each child! He is not just *any* child. He has special needs. You don't know how gifted he is and so vulnerable and scared."

Only after an hour of precious time and much determination do we *finally* come to a compromise. Although not giving them their request for Mrs. Green, I do promise to watch Sylvester personally and to make sure he is adjusting to this new setting. This I fully intend to do. He will experience many changes coming from a small private church school. I also have a nagging feeling that I will be encountering their pressure again.

SETTING THE OVERALL DISCIPLINE
CLIMATE FOR THE SCHOOL

When Sylvester's parents leave the office, a little fear comes over me about being in charge of a school facility, 487 children, and fifty-two staff members. But the children are mostly quiet, as is usual the first day. By the end of the week, however, I begin to see children running around the campus. I hear a few teachers yelling, "Sit down," as I walk by classrooms. I can tell that my expectations about conduct in this school are higher than those of some of my teachers. My highest priority needs to be establishing clear rules and expectations about discipline.

My rules are based on the knowledge of what I can tolerate from teachers and children. I believe that the climate of the school evolves from the standards, expectations, and consistency of the principal. Teachers have their personal classroom discipline, but the principal sets the tone for the whole campus. Schoolwide rules also can directly curb problems in the classrooms and give support to all the teachers.

Good instruction, naturally, is the biggest deterrent to misbehavior in the classroom. Ensuring that every classroom has good instruction will come only over time, as I support each teacher. In the meantime, I have to establish for the whole school certain rules of discipline that must be obeyed regardless of classroom teaching and classroom discipline.

BACKGROUND ON MY BELIEF ABOUT CHILDREN

For a few days I ponder my beliefs on disciplining children. There are certain "truths" about children that are at the very core of my being. Betsy and I examine these core values. *Children are people first, with rights the same as any human being. Second, all children seek consistency from authority figures and feel secure when lines of authority are established.*

As I try to figure out where my ideas come from, I am startled to realize that they arrived, very early in childhood, from my mother. Coming from a family of five daughters, with two sisters much older, I was babysitting my younger nephews and nieces by about the age of ten. My mother was a working mom and had very specific rules for us. She treated us with respect on our level and had very definite ideas about children. I can remember her saying, "Don't ever call children 'kids,' they are not baby goats, they are people just like us." We were never allowed to use the term *kids* in her presence. Years later, if I slipped in Mama's presence and called the children I was teaching "my kids," she immediately frowned and corrected me.

She used this example and many others in teaching us to become good babysitters. She always helped plan what we would do with the younger children for fun when we kept them. My mother gave us rules about what was acceptable behavior and what was unacceptable, as well as measures to apply in dealing with the children.

She never wavered in her rules and always listened and treated her children as people. Her measures were harsh and predictable. We knew exactly what to expect. The most hated consequence of our misbehavior was to have to stay "in the bathroom" for an hour, with absolutely no distractions. If we wanted to stay home from school sick, she would say, "Fine, but you know the rules. No reading, no TV, no radio, and you must just stay in the bed all day and rest." Needless to say, we did not fake illness and were really sick if we stayed home. But with all her rules, her most important influence was that we respected her and wanted her approval. We absolutely knew we could count on her to be fair.

When I started teaching first grade, the principle that children are to be treated as people was my mainstay, and it worked. I did not even know why at the time. Later, when I came to Florida, my principal came to me the first year I taught at his school. He said to me, "You know, Carolyn, you have a special way with children that I haven't seen very often. When you discipline them, you seem to be very fair, and they respond to what you are saying. You seem to have a knack for getting on their wavelength.

"I have watched you on the playground, in your classroom, and in the lunchroom, and I want to ask a favor. Because we have so many classrooms [1,200 children in a K–6 school], would you take over the major discipline problems for me in K–3 to ascertain what is happening? Of course, the teachers will have to make an appointment with you, when you have time, to talk with you about their discipline problem and then handle it. I want them to see your way of disciplining."

I answered: "Well, thank you for the compliment. Of course, I want to help all I can, but I still have my classroom to run. There is one way we might make it work. This school has a lot of student teachers. Would you give me one, as often as possible? I realize student teachers are a lot of work, but when he or she begins to help in the classroom, I will be a little more freed up to help with discipline. I will have another adult in the classroom if I get interrupted."

He agreed, and this was my first experience of disciplining children I did not teach. Luckily, we had very few real problem children at our school. The student teachers came every year for the next six years. This supervisor, from Florida Sate University, recommended that I become a professional reviewer for the State of Florida. Becoming a reviewer took me into the classrooms of teachers throughout the state who were having problems.

Over my tenure as peer teacher, curriculum resource teacher, professional reviewer, and assistant principal, I worked with over 200 teachers in improving instruction and discipline. So prior to being a principal, I had in my brain a catalog of clues to what was happening in a classroom. I could walk into a classroom and within five minutes tell if the teacher was being effective or not.

REASONING VERSUS RULES

A few years later, when working on a graduate degree, I studied Jean Piaget's work in more depth and learned about the developmental levels of children. In the early years of school, children are in the concrete operational stage and are not capable of abstract reasoning. So my gut feeling, when I hear a parent or a teacher using abstract reasoning language with a child, is consistent with Piaget's findings. When I see a parent trying to reason with a young child having a tantrum in a grocery store, I get the "fingernails across a chalkboard" reaction. I know that this child has not had boundaries set. Reasoning is not a substitute for clear rules and boundaries.

My mother's way of disciplining went along with Piaget. Children who have not yet developed abstract reasoning need to understand what the rules are for behavior, with many concrete examples. They need to know that there will be a consistent consequence when they break a rule. This training starts before a child is a year old and needs to be constant and unswerving.

During my graduate study I watched my teaching behavior carefully, to challenge Piaget's theory. I wanted to test this theory to be sure it was correct. I found myself critiquing what I did and said when I was in charge of children and the children's response to me. After a couple of years of being alert to this, the rules-and-consequences approach to discipline not only appeared to be what worked well but also seemed to help the children in their social development. It provides them with a sense of order in their world, which they need to begin developing abstract reasoning.

However, I do want to emphasize that no amount of rules, consequences, or planning can always succeed. We had some failures with our discipline program, but, by and large, the campus maintained emphasis on instruction every day. Many of the discipline problems we could not control were the fault of a teacher not being consistent.

Now that I am not in the capacity as principal anymore, I still find that children, in many different settings, gravitate to me and want to walk with me. This happens in all settings—at the grocery store, on a cruise ship, in church, anywhere that I have contact with children. I am real with them and can talk to them on their level regardless of age. I did not realize that this was special until my husband of fifteen years, a former professor of graduate students in education, began pointing it out to me with our grandchildren.

BEING REAL WITH CHILDREN

I have found that being real with children is contrary to much of what is espoused about reasoning with younger children. Not showing anger when disciplining them and keeping calm at all times are supposed to work in not giving children the wrong message. Contrary to this position, I firmly believe that children need to see and experience a wide range of emotions. This includes anger. By seeing an adult deal with anger in a very real, open, and constructive way, the child learns that anger is a normal reaction. I do not believe that children can learn to handle their emotions effectively if they do not see adults handle different emotions. Of course, some work is now being done in public education to help children understand their emotions. Programs have been produced to offer children different case scenarios and to show them how to react to emotions constructively.

I never get mad at a child and say anything that hits below the belt. By this I mean that I never say or imply, "You are a bad person." But I do raise my voice in anger; I do show my anger and disappointment and tell the child why. I am never angry at the children personally, but I am angry at their behaviors. I am very direct and just tell the child what I am feeling. I believe that this helps children to recognize anger in their own feelings and be able to cope with their feelings. Anger is just one emotion. The children I taught were also quick to recognize other emotions in me when they happened. If someone in our class experienced a loss of a loved one, then they saw my genuine sadness. I readily shared my feelings with my children when concrete examples presented themselves. This was only in a teaching capacity, of course, and I did not share my personal life or circumstances with them. I believe that, by doing this modeling, I helped children to cope better with their own emotions. You will see examples of my approach in several of the stories in this book.

RULES FOR THE CHILDREN AND THE TEACHERS

At the beginning of our first faculty meeting on rules for the campus, we explained and emphasized to the teachers certain assumptions that are my mainstay in dealing with children: *They are people first, with rights the same as any human being.* It is absolutely critical that children are treated with respect. This is evident in how a teacher talks with a child and teaches a child. This respect must be reflected throughout the campus by all staff members. *Second, all children seek consistency from authority figures.* Even though children will push the limits of the rules given them, we know that they do this for security within themselves. When firm rules are established and consistently enforced, children adjust and are happier. They love the security of knowing what they can and cannot do, and although they rebel, the rebellion is a test to see if you really love them.

Establishing with brevity and simplicity the rules to be used on the campus was critical for understanding and communication. After three meetings, the faculty and I agreed on four basic overall school campus rules:

1. Walk on campus—*no running allowed.* This meant walking between classrooms, coming to and from the cafeteria, in the mornings before school, going to the playground, or going to the bus. Running was allowed *only* during physical education and recess time. This rule was obviously for the safety of the children on campus. I only needed to recall my experience of seeing a broken bone protruding through a child's leg to imprint this rule on me for life!

2. Be kind. This includes two things: being respectful of authority and being kind to each other. Students have to be taught, daily, a frame of mind for dealing with other students. This rule took a long time to be implemented on the campus, between teachers and students, teachers

and parents, and all members of the school community. When I spoke I set the tone. This respectfulness had to be modeled at all times. I was especially adamant that teachers treat children as small human beings with the same respect as adults. Respect also involves the use of materials and equipment. So the teachers emphasized not only respect for others but also a respectful use of materials. The fact that our taxpayers pay for all these materials, textbooks, and equipment was stressed so the children could appreciate the money spent on their behalf.

3. Listen. This is a rule that is all-encompassing and complex. Listening is first demonstrated by the teachers in how they treat their students each day. Then the teachers begin teaching listening skills through the use of concrete audio examples (such as listening to tapes with sounds of airplanes, a door closing, a bicycle bell, etc.). After demonstrating listening and teaching children specifics about how to listen, the teacher models every day the behavior of listening carefully to another person—reminding students of what is being modeled. The teachers and I knew this would take a long time to teach. We all agreed to explain, model, and emphasize this skill throughout the campus. Again, my own example of careful listening was important every day in every communication. Few adults do listen very carefully. Some adults seem to be just waiting to talk instead of listening. By watching body language, I can usually tell if a person is listening.

4. No fighting. Anyone who fought on campus was taken home immediately. We experienced a lot of disruption from fights that first week. I absolutely forbade fighting, and *anyone* participating in a fight went home, no exceptions, irrespective of who started it. This rule caused me the most problems at first. Many children, especially those from rough neighborhoods, are taught at home that they must be able to protect themselves when out on the street. But after several months and *many, many* parent conferences, we were finally able to get the parents to understand that fighting causes a loss of instructional time for all children concerned, and this was not something we could afford.

The four rules were my mainstay as a principal, and we did not need more. They encompassed every aspect of dealing with disciplining children.

They also explained my actions to parents. Remaining *consistent* with these rules was the *absolute key* to success in implementing good discipline throughout the campus.

The rule posters looked like this:

School Rules
1. Walk
2. Be Kind
3. Listen
4. No Fighting

For clarity and emphasis, we posted our four rules throughout the campus on laminated 8½" × 11" colored construction paper. The signs were posted in every classroom and explained by the teacher. After this, I went to every classroom, explained the rules again, and answered questions. The children, teachers, and I created many possible scenarios to give examples of correct applications. We then sent a newsletter to the parents with a full explanation. All the children's homework that particular day, no matter what grade level, included taking the letter home, having it signed by a parent or guardian, and bringing back the signed part.

After these rules were in place, practiced, and, we hoped, understood by all the children, guidelines subsequently developed to cover sending a child to the principal's office for discipline reasons. The first guideline was about fighting. If children were in a fight, all parties to the fight were immediately sent to the office. I dropped everything, contacted the parents, and took the children home. If I could not find a parent, the child stayed in the office with me until time to go home. Then all participants in the fight were suspended from class for *three* days.

GUIDELINES FOR AN OFFICE REFERRAL

I knew from my administrative assistant that some teachers did not handle discipline adequately the previous year. Accordingly, we needed to establish restrictions concerning what the teacher had to do before a child could be sent to the office. Otherwise, a few teachers would send me all their discipline problems. The teachers and I set up a procedure for sending children to the office. Our plans included the following:

- Before a child could be sent to the office, for any problem other than fighting, the teacher had to have tried several interventions in the classroom. The first and most important intervention was to be sure that the child was being given assignments that were on the right instructional level for that child. I gave teachers many suggestions for on-level seat work and how it could be done.
- A second remedy was changing the seating arrangement of the child, to see if the child's misbehavior was being influenced by those around him or her.
- The third step was for the teacher to contact the parents about the behavior.

When a child was sent to the office for discipline reasons, I had a card on each child, alphabetized by surname, kept in the 3" × 5" card box on my desk. Every time a child was sent to me, I noted it and put the reason on the child's card. I then had the child sign the card, after we had discussed the situation, and filed the card. For all cases except fighting, my discipline rules for the office were as follows:

1. First time to the principal, have a conference: a "free" visit and warning. (About 70 percent of the children never reached #2.) The cards are my documentation.
2. Second time, the child's name goes into the discipline file, and the child signs his or her card. I make very sure the child understands that this is the final warning and that parents will be called on the third time. (Approximately 15 percent never reached #3.)
3. Third time, parents are called and told of all three offenses. (An additional 5 percent never reached level #4.)
4. Fourth time, the parents, teacher, and child must all meet with me in order for the child to be admitted back to class. (An additional 5 percent never reached #5.)
5. Fifth time, automatic suspension for three days. (An additional 3 percent never reached #6.)

6. Sixth time, I find the working parent and take the child to his or her job, and the child is suspended for five days. (I took two children to their parents at work.)

If the above are not adequate, as a last resort I would have the child spend at least one day alone in a room connected to my office with the door open with absolutely nothing to do all day but ponder his or her actions in the classroom. Most children were eager to try to remold their actions in the classroom. (Over my six-year tenure at Prescott, I had about twelve incidences of this nature.)

If a child continued to be a problem, I was left with no alternative but to keep suspending him or her. A child cannot legally pass a grade without a certain number of days of attendance, and I would caution the parents and the child each time another suspension was added. I hated to do this and do not remember any children who actually stayed back a year because of suspensions. Usually, after I met with the parents, teacher, and child (#4), we drew up a contract among all of us, and with the parent's cooperation, the improper behavior slowly went away.

ESTABLISHING THE CONSEQUENCES OF FIGHTING

The first fighting episode I had to deal with came the first week of school. Twin boys in Exceptional Student Education were being tormented by a big fifth grade boy. The three got into a fight. I immediately piled all three of them into my car and took them home. That was the first consequence of fighting.

If no adult was at home, I called the parents at work and had their child sit in the office with me for the day. I would automatically suspend all fighters for three days, with a note home to the parents or a phone call at night. When a fight happened, the children were not allowed back into the classroom, even if they had to spend the rest of the day sitting in a small conference room behind my office until their parents came home. In the first days of the new school year, I had as many as seven or eight children going home at one time.

I really did care about who started the fight, but I did not ask questions about who was at fault when it happened. Anyone who fought on the campus was automatically suspended for three days. When I found out what transpired to cause the fight, I later counseled with the noninstigating child and told the child that I knew he or she had not started the fight. My counsel to the students who did not start the fights was to follow the rule, not hit back, and tell a teacher. If the child said, "I told the teacher, but she didn't do anything," I would go to the teacher to ask her if she knew anything about this situation.

I hated to suspend children who were being mistreated, but I had to stop the fighting on campus. Any child who was in a fight had to stay out of school for three days. After about six weeks of school, fighting on campus was *very* rare. Parents, staff, and children all knew the consequences of fighting. I got some criticism from all sides, but I never wavered in this.

One white parent whose child got into a fight with a black child was especially enraged that I suspended both children. Mrs. Dayton huffed into my office one morning, out of control about her child and my fighting policy. She shouted in front of parents, children, and office staff that I was prejudiced against whites (using explicit derogatory language and profanity). I immediately coaxed her into my office (getting her out of the mainstream traffic).

She said, "I don't have to come into your office, just like I don't have to call you *Doctor Lawrence.*"

I answered, "No, you don't, but I will not speak with you out here." I walked into my office and held the door for her.

She was furious and said, "I have heard a lot about how you don't let children fight here at school. You are wrong. Children should be able to defend themselves. My Cynthia is in fourth grade and is doing great at Prescott. I encourage her to defend herself and her little sister, Betsy, in first grade. Now, that black girl was picking on Betsy, and she is in fifth grade. Cynthia has every right to step in and slap her face! That girl hurt Betsy, picked on her, and called her names. You are letting the black kids in this school take over. I am leaving right now to go to the superintendent. If you don't do a better job of looking after the white kids, I and some other parents will have your job!"

"Mrs. Dayton, I know you are upset, but I need for you to understand that I don't see color with children. All children who fight on campus, I suspend immediately. I can't have disruption of the school day. I must maintain a safe environment where *no child* can be hurt. Cynthia and all other children will benefit, in the long run, from this policy. I just want all children to get the best education they can get."

In a huff, she replied, "You, *Mrs.* Lawrence, are just prejudiced. I am going to the superintendent's office right now unless you take away Cynthia's suspension. She didn't cause the fight, she was protecting her sister, and I want her to keep protecting her! You will hear from the superintendent!"

I said, "Mrs. Dayton, you may want to call ahead. He is very busy. This is the superintendent's number." As I wrote the district number down for her, I said, "Please feel free to call him or anyone at the district office, if that will help you in dealing with me. My area director, who is my immediate supervisor, is Jack Waters. You may want to start with him."

I could tell by her body language that she was still in a rage as she left the school. Fortunately, for my own mental health, I was too busy to dwell on what might happen. I had a school to run and needed to be visible throughout the day for all the children and teachers. So I left the office and started visiting different areas in the school.

After about an hour of handling other problems, such as a hot water heater in the cafeteria going on the blink, I got a beep on my pager to come to the office. My secretary was agitated as she told me that the superintendent's secretary was on the phone. "Hi, Ann. What's the trouble? Has Mrs. Dayton reached you yet?"

The superintendent's secretary said, "Reached me! Reached me! She is standing in the front office screaming profanities, in shorts and barefooted, and won't leave until she talks to Dr. Smith. He is in a board meeting right down the hall, and I am sure all the board members can hear her. She is acting like a raving maniac! What is going on with her?"

I explained all the details to Ann about what transpired that morning. We decided on the strategy of getting her to talk to my area director, Jack Waters, right then, because he was available. He is a former principal and has a very calming affect on everyone he meets. I knew he would support me but, at the same time, would have suggestions about how I could defuse the situation.

Within an hour I received a call from my area director. He told me that he had gotten Mrs. Dayton to calm down somewhat and had told her to contact me the next day. He suggested that I figure out some ways to win her over to my side. I got the same advice from my husband that night at home. Winning her over was my very last choice of what I wanted to do to her! But I knew I had to do it. How could I ever get her on my side?

I decided to let things calm down a little. I did not hear from her the next day. On Wednesday, without mentioning the incident in the office, I called and asked her advice about two community issues. I also asked her to consider being on my school advisory board. I gave her some background for this job and asked that she come to school the following week and shadow me in my job for two days. She was an at-home mother with her children in school, and she agreed to this.

When she arrived on Monday, she seemed a different person. She was dressed nicely, clean, calm, and a little excited about being called by the principal to come and help the school. We spent the next two days together, all day long, and she was enthralled with all that happened with parents and the children. She saw everything, though I steered her away from classroom instructional problems and teacher conferences.

At the end of the two days she told me she had not had any idea about the responsibilities of a principal. She was in awe of all the problem solving needed every day. She even told me that she could understand why I had to suspend children for fighting and would support me!

She was especially specific about how busy my days were and cautioned me that I *must* take time to eat lunch every day to keep up my strength! I could not believe the difference in this woman, and I was very proud of her turnaround. I could count on her as a positive voice in the community instead of a negative one! Thank goodness for the good advice given to me by my district supervisor!

PRACTICAL CONSEQUENCES OF FIGHTING

My teachers and I had several meetings about the fighting rule. We knew that in a community where children needed to protect themselves, fighting was sometimes necessary for survival. It is very hard to teach not to fight back. The only way we could control this on the campus was to say that the school campus was different from real life. We definitely did not want to destroy what the parents had taught the children about surviving on the street.

Every day we continued to work to differentiate between neighborhood environment and school environment. We had a few parents who never agreed with us and just got mad. For example, there was Anthony's mom, who walked into my office after school hours. I had been unable to contact her during the day, and Anthony had spent the day in the office. She said to Anthony, ignoring me completely, "Well, did you win?" He replied, "Yeah, mom, I won." "Okay, then, let's go get you anything you want to eat, for a reward!" As she walked out of the office she smirked at me and said, "As long as my child is winning his fights, I don't care what you say at school. I want my child to be strong and be able to protect himself." I sighed with frustration as she left with Anthony and could only hope that she would eventually teach him to adhere to the rules. If not, Anthony would spend a lot of time suspended from school. I also worried that he would not respect authority, which might hurt him as a teenager or adult.

Although we met with defeat with a few parents, we still adhered to the rule each time. While I understood and empathized with what Anthony's mom was saying, we knew we could not give children a good education without instilling respect for authority. Without this ironclad rule, much instructional time would be lost. Time for instruction was very valuable to all of us. Three days of suspension each time could really cause an inconvenience for the parents and reduce academic progress for the children.

A DIFFERENT DISCIPLINE PROBLEM

Terri, Sharon, and Cassandra were brought to the office for breaking the "Be Kind" rule. The teacher, a very reserved, superior teacher, told me that they were charging younger girls money to get into the restroom.

I could not believe it! Terri, who had repeated two grades, was about an inch taller than I am (and I am 5'9") and would intimidate almost anyone because of her large frame. Cassandra was a gregarious character, full of life and engaging. Sharon was a sweet, plump, "follow the group" kind of girl. These three girls already had a reputation, from past years, as bullies.

They had a kind of clique that I had already noticed. Being in the fifth grade made them special because they were the oldest on the campus. I knew I had to nip this in the bud to establish authority. They were already undesignated leaders among the fifth graders.

My first statement to them was, "I have heard of some bad behavior on campus, but this is probably among the worst. Aren't you familiar with the *laws* of going to school in this district? There is a book that gives the laws and rights of students! If you don't follow this law, then you can be expelled from public school, and your parents will have to pay for a private school. That is about $250 per month for each of you." Then I got down a professional-looking book and improvised: *"'Each student in the school will have the right of protection and safety on the school campus. Any student threatening another student or bribing another student will be treated as a criminal, with the same laws governing them that govern young adults. Punishment will be immediate and without hesitation.'*

"Well, girls, let me hear your side of the story. I wish I could help you more, but it looks as if you have stepped over the line this time. I don't know that I can save you from court action. You probably will not be able to keep coming to Prescott Elementary."

Cassandra said, "Oh, Dr. Lawrence, we didn't know this was a serious crime. We were just playing and thought it would be fun."

"Fun? You call it 'fun' to charge a child to go to the restroom? Have you every heard of the term *extortion*? That is what you did. How would *you* feel if you had to go to the restroom and didn't have any money and someone *bigger and older* than you was standing there charging money? You are fifth graders and the leaders of this school. All the other students look up to you. Anyway, I am not able to overturn the law. I have to follow it."

With this, I picked up the phone and dialed the police (actually calling the time of day) and said, "Officer, I have three girls here that I have to report. They are charging younger girls to go to the restroom. I know I have to report this to the police and. . . . No, *sir,* I didn't know it was *that* serious. But, sir, these are really good girls, basically; they just didn't know what they were doing. Couldn't we just give them one more chance? Please, I have looked at their records here at school. They have been bullies for a few years but have made passing grades. Because they are just in the fifth grade, could we please treat them as not quite adults yet? What can they do to keep from going to court?"

I listened very carefully to the imaginary officer on the phone and then promised that we would comply with all rules to rectify the situation. By this time, the girls were looking at me with wide-eyed fear.

"Well, girls. You have one chance to avoid going to court. Do you think you know who you charged?"

"Oh, yes, Dr. Lawrence. We'd only just started when Mrs. Fisher caught us. We didn't take money from very many children, and they were all third graders. We will give the money back!"

"Well, the officer said if you can make things right, then maybe, *this time,* you can get by with apologizing. But you know, if *anything* happens like this again, I will have to call your parents in, tell them about this, and call the police again. You know I can't protect you just because I like you as individuals and think you are basically good girls."

"Oh, Dr. Lawrence, if you would just help us this one time, we will *never* do it again. We promise. We don't want you to tell our mothers about this— we will be in *deep* trouble, and we promise to be good!"

"Okay, then. Let's go to the class, find the girls, and let you talk with them."

IMPLEMENTING MY RECORD OF REFERRALS

Before the girls went to the third grade class, I recorded their offense on each child's card and had them sign their individual cards. I explained carefully that the first time in the office was between each child and me. I did not call or tell the parents. This way, I hoped to stem the number of repeaters to the office and to give all children a second chance just between the two of us. I explained that their second time in the office I would have to call their parents and tell them about the first and second offenses. The third time in the office, the child would be sent home for three days.

After this, I took the three girls with me, and we went to Mrs. Fisher's class for the girls to apologize. I went into the classroom and talked to the whole class about what had happened. I told them about this being *very serious* and said that all the children on our campus had rights as citizens. Then I asked for a show of hands of the girls who were charged. Three girls raised their hands, and I called them outside with Terri, Cassandra, and Sharon. The guilty girls apologized profusely, handed over some coins to the girls, and promised *never* to do such a thing again. The third graders returned to class.

"Okay, girls, you can go back to class. Remember that 'Be Kind' means treating other students with respect and not violating individuals' rights. I don't expect to ever see you three in my office again. This is a special exception for you to get this second chance. If I ever hear of anything like this again, you know I won't take up for you twice."

As the girls walked away I heard Cassandra say, "*Whew,* man, that Dr. Lawrence, she don't play. Man, I didn't think we were going to get out of there without being picked up."

Terri replied, "Oh, she ain't so tough, and I wasn't scared. I don't think we could go to jail either, just maybe the police would come out to see about us."

Cassandra and Sharon just looked at her hard. "Man," Sharon said, "do you know how my mom would beat my butt if the *police* had to come out here about me?"

I just smiled to myself and knew that these three would be wary before doing this type of thing again. I suspected that this was not the end of this little dynasty, though.

SYLVESTER, THE PRIVATE SCHOOL CHILD

In the third week of school, Sylvester, the Van Astor's first grader from a private school, was brought to my office for hitting Amanda. I had checked on his well-being every day, as I had promised his parents. For the first week of school, I made sure he was comfortable by eating with him in the crowded lunchroom.

The teacher, Mrs. Blalock, said that Amanda refused to give Sylvester her potato chips at lunch, and he hit her. I was sure there had been a mistake and brought him into my office. He admitted taking the potato chips but said he did not hit Amanda.

Sylvester and I revisited very carefully the discipline rules for coming to the office. Then I asked Sylvester about his class and his experience with Prescott. He told me that he was happy with his classmates and his teacher. He said that he had a good first three weeks and loved public school. Because this was his first offense, I explained why taking someone's property is a very serious problem and had him sign his card in the office. Then I took him to apologize to Amanda.

Within a week, Sylvester was brought back for his second offense. He had called Fred a bad word in front of the whole class. I asked: "Exactly what did Sylvester say?" Mrs. Blalock said, "He called Fred a 'shit ass.'" Shocked, I mentally shook my head. Now, wait a minute, I thought, was this Sylvester, the son of those parents who said he is a good Christian boy who behaves? I directed Mrs. Blalock to leave Sylvester with me.

"Sylvester, I'm sure this must be a mistake. Will you tell me about this?"

"Yes, ma'am. I didn't say those bad words. Mrs. Blalock just said I did. I wouldn't *ever* say those kinds of words!" He looked at me so innocently that I was momentarily confused and went to question Mrs. Blalock.

"Dr. Lawrence, I've been teaching seventeen years, and I have yet to 'frame' a child. But don't take my word for it. Just ask any of the children in the class. He said it in front of everyone."

Mustering as much calmness and poise as I could under her blistering glare, I asked a child, at random, to come outside with me. Her name tag said "Susie." "Susie, did you hear Sylvester say any bad words today?"

Susie had big brown eyes and a face that was anxious to please. "Yes, ma'am. I heard him say 'shit ass' to Fred."

Susie went back into the room quietly, and I motioned for a boy in the back of the room to come and speak with me. This boy's name was Eric. "Eric, did you hear Sylvester say any bad words?" "Yes, ma'am, he said 'shit ass' right there in class!"

Both children were thrilled to have been given "license" to say the bad words. I hated the fact that I had them repeated, and I was infuriated with Sylvester. He lied to me while appearing so innocent. I was also mad with myself for not handling the situation better. I did not like interrupting the teacher but knew that I needed to support my documentation. I certainly wanted my teachers to know that I backed them in these difficult situations. Still, I did have to give due process to Sylvester. I rushed back to my office, giving my secretary a warning not to stop me for any message. I slammed my office door behind me, glaring at Sylvester.

"What in the world do you mean, young man, telling me a story about not saying bad words? I just talked with your teacher and two of your classmates, and they told me you did say the bad words. I won't stand for this kind of be-havior. You were in here last week for taking Amanda's potato chips, and I gave you your one chance. Now you have gotten into trouble for saying the bad words and *then* not telling me the truth. *And* I am going to call your parents right now and tell them about this."

Sylvester looked at me calmly and said, "No, ma'am, I didn't say those words."

Furiously I dialed his father at work, left a message, and directed Sylvester to wait in my office. Within an hour, Dr. Van Astor was at the school. "I got a message that Sylvester is in some trouble. What seems to be the problem?"

Bringing Sylvester and Dr. Van Astor into my office, I quietly closed the door. "Sylvester, tell your father why you are in trouble."

"I don't know. Mrs. Blalock says I said some bad words, but I didn't. Everybody is always picking on me. I didn't do anything."

Frankly, I was openmouthed at this child's outright lie to his father. I gave Sylvester a withering look and then went over with the father all my actions. I explained about calling the children out of the classroom to verify what Sylvester had said.

"Dr. Lawrence, Sylvester is a Christian. If he says he didn't say those words, I believe him. I don't even have to ask him if he is telling the truth. He has never lied to us."

I ushered Sylvester out of the office to wait for his father. I returned to Dr. Van Astor. "Dr. Van Astor, Sylvester has been to the office twice in the first three weeks of school. He signed this note that he admitted he took part of a child's lunch without permission. How do you think the children came up with the same story about Sylvester and his language when I had them come outside of the room to tell me about what had happened?"

Dr. Van Astor replied: "I know Sylvester doesn't lie. If he said he didn't say those words, I believe him. Maybe he needs to change to Mrs. Green's classroom where we wanted him at the first of school and then maybe he won't get picked on."

I remained totally calm and professional, but I was frustrated. "No, I'm not changing his classroom. And Sylvester has got to behave. I suspend children when they continue to get into trouble."

"You are the principal, and we are his parents. We have *much more* experience with Sylvester than you have. We know how truthful he is, and I will not allow him to be suspended. Someone or something besides Sylvester is causing this problem."

I replied, "I know Sylvester has done these two things. He has broken school rules. If he doesn't suffer consequences for his bad behavior, it will get worse. The other children will wonder what happened. I can't allow this type of behavior to interrupt children's learning, including Sylvester's. I want us to work together and try to get to the bottom of this."

We disagreed for about ten minutes. I remained adamant. Sylvester would be disciplined according to school rules. Dr. Van Astor said, "I will just call your area director at the district office!" I calmly gave him my supervisor's name and number and told him to be my guest. I did not ever hear from the district about Sylvester, and he did have to apologize to the class.

Two months passed, and Sylvester was in my office again. Mrs. Blalock came in the office looking like death. She was visibly shaking. "Dr. Lawrence, I don't want you to get upset, but I just found Sylvester, Billy, and Joanne naked in my storage closet."

"*What? Naked!* Why were they in the closet long enough to get naked?"

"Well, I put them in there for being bad, and they closed the door and turned off the light. To tell you the truth, I forgot they were in there, but don't get upset."

"Mrs. Blalock, you *know* that children are never left unsupervised. That is so dangerous for them and for you, legally. Just have them come immediately to my office, and I'll talk to you later."

The three children came sheepishly into the office, shuffling their feet and looking at the floor as they closed the door.

"Mrs. Blalock just told me you three took off all your clothes in the closet!"

Billy said, "Uh-uh—we did not. We left our shoes on."

Tears began to stream down Joanne's face. In spite of the seriousness of the situation, Billy's response about leaving their shoes on almost made me laugh out loud, even though I was horrified! At the same time, I was thinking, *What am I going to tell these parents?* I thought of a lawsuit. *Help!*

"I *cannot* believe that you three had to be put into the closet in the *first place*. Whatever were you thinking of, taking off all your clothes? I know you left shoes on, but they aren't clothes."

Sylvester very earnestly explained, "Well, I just started to bend my belt over like this." He showed me, taking his hands and bending his belt to show the inside, "and then we kinda really got bored, so Billy said, 'Let's turn off lights.' So we did, and then Joanne said, 'Let's take off all our clothes,' and so we did."

"Sylvester, if someone asked you to jump into a fire and burn yourself, would you do it? I am talking about serious stuff here. Children are not allowed to get naked in this school. This is so against the rules that I can't even *decide* how bad the punishment should be. I can't believe the very serious trouble the three of you are in."

They truly began to look scared. Not wanting to experience this unique situation alone, I told them to wait right there and called my curriculum resource teacher, Mrs. Greatsy.

"Mrs. Greatsy, I want you to be a witness to this terrible thing that has happened in Mrs. Blalock's room. Billy, Sylvester, and Joanne just pulled off all their clothes in the closet in their room because they didn't have anything else to do."

We could hardly keep straight faces, but this was very serious. Mrs. Greatsy was very troubled by the news and parroted my expression of horror and disbelief. I told the children to wait right there, and we went out into the hallway to conference.

I said, "This is very serious for Mrs. Blalock. Obvious neglect of the children, I can't believe it!" Even though it was such a serious issue, we looked at each other and dissolved into helpless laughter over children who were six years old and did this type of thing out of boredom. Six-year-old children are innocent about sex. They really were just trying something different. We commiserated about how we could never tell what was going to happen on any given day, we laughed some more, and then she departed for other conferences.

I decided to handle this delicately. Dr. and Mrs. Van Astor told me that Sylvester *never* lied and always told them when he had done something wrong. Well, I thought, this time we will have a test.

I went back into my office and said: "Okay, this is what I want you three to do. I want you *all* to tell your parents what happened and ask them to come to see me tomorrow. This is so serious that I think part of your punishment should be to tell them. I am going to give each of you a letter today to take home and return to me tomorrow, signed by your parents. In the letter I am asking your parents to come to school tomorrow morning to talk with me."

They all agreed immediately. Sylvester was *especially* eager for this reprieve. Joanne and Billy seemed more hesitant about telling their parents than Sylvester.

Sure enough, the next morning, as I suspected, Joanne's mother and Billy's parents were in the office when I came back from making my rounds of the classrooms. Sylvester's parents were nowhere to be seen. I knew he had not told them.

I had a long conference with the parents and promised that Mrs. Blalock would be disciplined for not watching the children more carefully. I then emphasized that children this age really were just *playing*, and this did not need to be discussed anymore. I punished the children for misbehaving by having them tell their parents. But I emphasized that the thought of being naked was not connected, in the children's minds, to any sexual act. The parents were dismayed but reassured and did not overreact. We decided on punishment at home but no more at school, and they left, with my assurance that this type of action on the part of any teacher in this school would *never* happen again.

I did not hear from Sylvester's parents, so I decided to go see Sylvester. I found him on the playground and called him over to me. "Sylvester, did you tell your parents about what happened yesterday?"

"Oh, yes, ma'am. They said that was all right. They understood and were not upset. I just shouldn't ever do that again."

"Sylvester, did you give them the letter?"

"Yes, ma'am, they just didn't want to sign it."

"Okay, Sylvester, I am so glad you told them. I would hate to think that you didn't tell them. Joanne's mom and Billy's parents came to see me this morning, and we talked it over. Don't you think your parents would like to come in about it?"

"Well, they would, but they are busy and said they would take care of it."

"Okay, Sylvester. If you are really telling me the truth. You know your parents trust you. But I think I'll call them to be sure."

For the rest of the day, as I had time, I constantly tried to contact Sylvester's parents. Finally, I got them, and they agreed to a conference late that afternoon after work hours. I agreed to keep Sylvester in my office after school until they got there.

We spent over an hour discussing exactly what happened, with Sylvester, as usual, saying that he was not the instigator but, rather, just went along with the other children. The fact that he did not get home with the letter, however, was one fact that the parents could not explain. I showed the letters signed by the other two parents and then told them that they had come to the school that morning. The Van Astors, finally, began to look uncomfortable.

Of course, I took major responsibility for this happening in the school. Ultimately, I was responsible for everything that happened to each child. I had assured all the parents that the teacher had already been taken from the classroom and assigned by the district staff as an aide at another school. When they left the school, I was somewhat reassured that they were beginning to realize that Sylvester was capable of being a six-year-old child with some negative behavior. Luckily, they did not mention that they had requested another first grade teacher, Mrs. Green, several times. I knew by this omission on their part in our conversation that they were unsettled and unhappy with Sylvester.

After about five weeks of enforcing rules and adhering to procedures, the number of referrals to the office decreased dramatically. I could tell that the children had begun to settle down into a routine. I thought I could begin to spend part of my day in the classrooms observing and helping with instruction. Over the past week, I had observed many instances that made me question what was happening in certain classrooms. So I talked with my office staff and planned my days with one hour a day in classes.

4

IRONING OUT OUR EXPECTATIONS FOR INSTRUCTION

This chapter addresses the process of identifying specific instructional plans for the year and beginning to put them into practice. The faculty and I spent much time on narrowing the instructional focus to reading, without slighting other subjects. I gave individual teachers demonstration teaching, and the teachers gave each other input in faculty meetings on the effective ways they had found to teach reading. Together we were also able to set clear expectations for formal evaluations for the year.

TODAY'S NIGHTMARE ABOUT TEST SCORES

Teaching that is geared to achievement tests is currently a priority at most schools. As an assistant principal for instruction, curriculum resource teacher, and principal, I saw many schools spend so much time emphasizing test scores and practicing for accountability tests that many activities promoting the love of learning were squeezed out.

Newspaper reports of statewide test scores, school by school, have the effect of ranking one school against another and stepping up the pressure on students and teachers alike. Many schools, I think *most schools,* have become pressure cookers for good test scores, making school life less satisfying for all concerned. I know that many of my friends who were my best, most productive teachers have left or are leaving the profession because of the preoccupation with testing. This is especially true in schools with predominantly low-income students, where children are more disadvantaged, with many being developmentally slow. This is where our best teachers are most urgently needed. When a school is labeled as a *D* or *F* school, the teachers typically get demoralized, and enthusiasm wanes.

Just before writing this chapter I talked with a teacher who was one of the most inspiring teachers I met in my thirty-two years in education. She is voluntarily in one of the most poverty-ridden sections of her school district. Sadly, she is leaving education because of the pressure of test scores and accountability.

When I expressed my dismay and told her what a loss this would be to our children and their education, she replied: "Thanks for the good words. But, Carolyn, you don't understand. Teaching is not what it used to be. I am not allowed to have that special 'corner with a carpet piece' where a child can sneak away and read quietly on the floor. I am not allowed to spend a day celebrating an author or having the children dress up as characters in a book. We are under so much pressure because of accountability testing that many days are just drill, drill, drill. The children's eyes glaze over with practicing the skills they will be tested on. There is so much more to learning than the testable skills. The children don't love to come to school anymore. As a professional educator, I literally cannot stand what I am required to do to my children.

"You know I love teaching all levels of elementary school because of the children's enthusiasm for learning. This is what has kept me going when outside obstacles get in my way. Now I can see children in first, second, and third grades who already hate to come to school."

I want to scream with frustration when I talk with these special people. I wish superintendents, principals, parents, and teachers would rise up together and rebel because of the unfair rankings of different populations of children. But when administrators and parents do not support teachers in their professional judgment of what is best for their children's learning, these talented teachers are responding by leaving the profession in large numbers.

LAYING THE GROUNDWORK FOR GOOD
TEST SCORES AND GOOD INSTRUCTION

I do believe there are ways to have high test scores *and* to foster high-quality and enjoyable instruction that also promote the love of learning. Test scores were already an issue by the time I became a principal, but the pressures were not as stifling as they are today. To have the Prescott Elementary teachers trust me as an instructional leader, I assured them that test scores would not drive our curriculum, *period.* I would serve as a buffer for them from state and district pressure to put the test at the center of our work. We would not teach to the test. We would use instructional strategies proven by research, primarily those already familiar to the teachers.

I had just finished my doctoral degree in curriculum and instruction, and I was steeped in the research on effective instruction. I gained so much from my instructional leadership program and its exceptional professors that I was very confident I could put into practice what I had learned from the research. I was conscious of the findings that showed that effective schools focused on just a very few goals at a time, constantly keeping them in awareness. We would choose goals that were consistent with what the teachers were already doing. And we would emphasize these goals each day, instead of emphasizing drilling for a test.

I explained to my teachers three sets of research findings: time on task, correct instructional level in reading, and the critical linkage among achievement, individual practice work assignments, and self-esteem. Then we agreed to focus these practices specifically on the teaching of reading. This became our instructional mission, and we expected to keep this focus for at least two years.

Over the next couple of years this narrow focus was most important, for in the elementary grades the ability to read was paramount. By narrowing the focus we felt we could get to know the level of each child and ensure that he or she was learning to read.

I cautioned the teachers that we could not expect our scores to go up quickly if we were implementing these practices correctly. Taking time to implement good practices, to carefully find out the level of each child in reading and to match instruction to the child's level in reading seat work assignments, would invariably lead to improved test scores—but not for at least a year.

Most of the instructional staff understood why I wanted to make reading instruction the first priority of our improvement plan. While we worked on improving instruction through correct teaching practices, I promised I would be responsible to the district staff and to the parents if our test scores did not go up or actually went down temporarily.

I brought my supervisor into the loop concerning what we wanted to do at our school. This would involve finding the correct reading instruction level for each child, placing the children in classrooms by stratified random assignment rather than by ability, and then teaching them in reading groups at the correct instructional level. This plan would also involve making sure every child was successful every day in his or her practice-reading seat work.

I further explained to the teachers that for the first couple of years these two items, children being on the correct reading level and having correct seat work, would be the only two categories I would be evaluating in their instruction. For these formal evaluations I would visit their rooms at a pre-arranged time, to review only reading instruction and seat work. My other visiting times would not be for evaluation but simply for me to view different kinds of academic instruction and give help where it was needed.

BACKGROUND WORK DURING THE SUMMER

Before school started I read each child's individual cumulative folder. I made a poster chart for each grade with the children's names ranked by reading level. This gave me some preliminary data for dividing the children into classroom sections. To gain additional information on the correct reading level, Betsy, my administrative assistant, and I ordered placement tests corresponding to the reading series books in use at our school. When the teachers arrived in the fall, I got their support in giving these placement tests during the first week of school.

After comparing my list from the cumulative folders with the results of the placement tests, we adjusted the classroom assignments of some children to ensure that each teacher had only three reading levels to manage. In practical terms, the stratified random assignment of students meant sorting students by grade level and reading level and from those classifications assigning them randomly to teachers. Most teachers were very pleased with the idea of having self-contained classrooms and having only three levels to teach in reading.

After we knew the placement levels of all the children in first through fifth grade, Betsy and I made a central book room for all reading materials. These materials included everything the teachers needed for proper reading instruction. We included teachers' editions, student workbooks, large teaching charts for each reading level, and all supplementary material in the reading series. We also ordered, for each grade level, one phonics workbook, not in the reading series, that I knew was particularly effective. As soon as the children were placed permanently in their classrooms, the teachers were given their reading texts and supplementary materials according to the groupings in their room.

Having the central book room saved our school money. Rather than equipping each classroom separately with a set of appropriate books, we supplied books as needed when teachers turned in test results showing that the students were ready to move up to the next level. Of course, the workbooks had to be written in, and the children, when finishing the workbooks, took them home.

The system of the central book room provided a bonus for Betsy and me. When the teachers checked out books, we now had the means to track each child's progress. When parents called about a problem, I could reassure them that I was on top of the instructional situation of their child. I could consult my charts and tell the parents the reading level of their child, assure them that the child's instruction was on that level, and explain that we had a way of tracking the child's progress and success every day.

Parents loved the fact that I was in the classroom often. Realistically, I could not check each child's reading every week, but I rotated through classrooms and spot-checked the children's progress by the teacher's lesson plans. Twice a month teachers gave me a copy of their lesson plans for the coming two weeks, listing page numbers and books for each reading group and the other subjects. When I was working in classrooms and when I read report cards before they went home, I had my reference charts on my office wall to be sure each child was progressing.

I also used the charts when a discipline problem arose. When teachers sent children to my office for disciplinary reasons, they also sent along the practice work the child was doing that day. The charts allowed me to see if the practice work was on the correct level for the child. These charts also gave me credibility with the teachers, showing that I was committed to helping them improve instruction, informing parents about the children's needs, and fo-cusing on our main goal of success in reading for every child.

THE LAST PIECE OF THE PUZZLE ABOUT READING

The last step, besides implementing the reading series, involved asking the teachers in first through fifth grades to use the phonics workbooks every day for a fun activity and review. The phonics workbooks we ordered for the whole school were purchased by the Parent Teacher Association. We did this because they were not on the state-adopted reading list, but I knew that they were excellent. They cost about $2.00 per child. The workbook as-signed to the whole class was one grade level below the grade they were cur-rently in. In order words, we ordered second grade phonic books for all third graders. The students did not know, of course, that the activities were one grade level below them. The books (published by Modern Curriculum Press) were attractive and colorful, containing fun activities for the children that provided practice and reinforcement in skills they had already learned. They all included such things as connect the dots, mazes, figure–ground perception, and many additional skills suitable for whole-group instruction.

By having students use their workbooks every day, I could ensure that children who had gaps in phonics were being helped with the review. The children who already knew the material were not bored because the pages were different from their other materials, and they were attractive and fun. Because seat work is supposed to be mastered at a rate of 85 to 90 percent accuracy, I knew that the review would hurt none of the children, and this practice-to-mastery would be a good investment of our precious instruction time.

I held a demonstration lesson on the *pace* for teaching the phonics book for the chairperson's class in each grade. This was to show teachers how fast to go with the children, how to correct the papers as a group, and how to be alert to those who needed extra help. Then all the chairpersons showed their teachers. In this way, there could be no mistake about how to move through this material at a brisk pace. The teachers appreciated taking this fun break with the whole class and loved the materials. This made for an enjoyable, in-formal time for everybody.

PROBLEMS FOR A FIRST GRADER

Even with all the care we took to place students in reading groups on their level, we had several who were misplaced and needed individual attention. Mrs. Watson came to me about Tony, a big first grader with huge brown cow eyes and absolutely no clue about foundation skills and no love of reading. He was beginning to be a discipline problem in the classroom. He lived with his grandparents and had no help with letters, sounds, or colors.

Mrs. Watson brought him to the office, left him outside in the front office, and said, "Dr. Lawrence, I haven't a clue what to do about Tony. He is larger than the other children and uses this weight and height to pick on smaller children. He cuts up in the classroom all the time, and I suspect he is going to get worse as the year goes by. I have talked with his grandparents. His parents are out of the picture and left Tony with them when he was only a year old. They haven't seen or heard from the parents since. They have reared nine other children and are just worn out with Tony. But the grandmother is anxious to help any way she can."

When I brought Tony into the office, he looked at me with eyes full of mischief and calculating how he could manage to get out of this situation. "Tony, what seems to be the problem in your class? Mrs. Watson tells me that you are giving her trouble when she is trying to teach."

"This school is just dumb. I don't want to be in school, and nobody likes me in the whole class."

I replied, "Tony, how about staying with me for a while, and let's do some work and see if we can make school a little better."

I told Mrs. Watson that I wanted to screen Tony on a lower scale than the reading series placement tests. Specifically, I wanted to know which letters and sounds, particularly which vowel sounds, he knew, decoding words with the use of primary grade phonics. To further complicate Tony's problem, when I gave Tony a self-esteem inventory, I found that his self-esteem was extremely low and that he was antagonistic about even trying to learn to read. I knew that we had to build his self-esteem in ways other than reading instruction.

When I had a conference that afternoon with Mrs. Watson, she was amazed at what Tony did not know and agreed that we needed to build his self-esteem rather than keep pressuring him about reading. She decided that she would help him by using a health lesson and give him positive strokes in other areas. He was normal in math concepts and did well. She used a health project to measure the children individually and, sure enough, found that Tony was top for height in the class. She did several projects to ensure that Tony's self-esteem was enhanced and told me that he began to feel better about himself.

Before the end of each day, late in the afternoon, Mrs. Watson would work with Tony. I would help her when I could get to her class. Together we did readiness skills such as learning nursery rhymes, learning beginning and ending sounds, and using many fun books for the appreciation of reading. She or I used motivational picture books with great illustrations for about fifteen minutes at a time. Each day she had a child go to the library with Tony and read him fun literature.

Little by little, Tony's self-esteem—as evidenced by his posture and self-confidence in class—gradually began to improve. At first, Mrs. Watson told me she would only ask him questions in class that she knew he could answer. Gradually, using very small steps in the reading process, she put him into a small group of children near his level and made him successful every day. She knew that teaching developmentally slow students means two steps forward, most times, and one step back. Progress was very slow.

At the end of thirteen weeks, she called me to her class. Tony was still tentative about reading, but his self-esteem had improved dramatically! He learned enough to want to read out loud to the class. He read a "Big Book" (these are books that measure about 3' × 3', have very few words, and show great illustrations; they are a treat for the whole class).

Somehow Tony equated good reading with *loud* reading, and when he read, he read at the *top of his lungs*! His voice carried over the entire class. He was so pleased to have learned some of the tricks of recognizing words that he wanted everyone to know! The teacher did not correct the loudness of his reading, and the other children were kind.

Mrs. Watson asked me later to show her how I found the specific correct instructional level for Tony. I told her that I had basically made a handmade test for recognizing beginning and ending sounds. I added short and long vowel sounds, and last I made up nonsense words to be sure children could decode words. Then, as a first grade teacher, I would have a good idea of what children did or did not know.

Letter Recognition and Sounds

Below is a reconstruction of what I gave to Mrs. Watson:

Child's Name: _____

Recognition of Letters: [Child names the letters to you as you use a duplicate copy of the test to mark mistakes, without the child seeing you mark the paper.]

See how many of these capital letters you can name for me:

Z B C X P A S Y I D U M O

L F V H N J Q E I G R K W

See how many of these lowercase letters you can name for me:

w b r z k c g z i x e p q a

j s n y h t v d f u l d o m

Have you ever heard of a letter called a vowel?

Can you name the five long vowel sounds?

a e i o u

Do you know the names of these short vowels?

a e i o u

Can you sound out any of these play words?

pud hiz lop wez fis cume tobe sole mote

After using this short screening test, which takes about ten minutes, the teacher knows if a child has had any contact with letter names or letter sounds. These basic essentials are necessary to get a child started in reading. Words memorized to begin reading only go into a child's short-term memory, and the child loses these words easily. Understanding sounds and using them to break down a word are much longer-term memory skills.

The teacher was very pleased to have this short screening device at her fingertips, and I am sure many teachers all over the country in kindergarten and first grade use a similar screening of some kind. The self-esteem inventory is not as commonly used but is particularly helpful for major discipline problems. I used the "Coopersmith Self-Esteem Inventory" from Consulting Psychology Press in California. Of course, I had to get approval from Tony's grandmother for this, and I talked with her about the results.

Tony was very lucky and worked hard. At the end of the year, I made sure he was assigned one of our best second grade teachers, and he improved enough in reading to be an average reading student by the end of third grade.

His discipline problems diminished as his self-esteem improved, and the teacher and I truly believed that his confidence in reading was the major factor.

VISITING THE CLASSROOMS INFORMALLY

I began the process of informal classroom visits during the first six weeks of school, to get the children comfortable with my presence in the rooms. By visiting classrooms often to say hello, deliver messages, or just compliment the class on good behavior, I became a familiar presence to teachers and students. In addition, over a six-week period I gave each teacher a thirty-minute break to work in the classroom while I read to the children. I used the same two wonderful books for each session, no matter the grade level: Shel Silverstein's *Where the Sidewalk Ends* and Mercer Meyer's *There's a Nightmare in My Closet*. I continued this practice as often as I could throughout the year. The children asked me for specific poems by Silverstein, and at times we even recited them together because they were so funny.

After about six weeks, with everything finally in place, I told the teachers that I would be making nonevaluative, helping visits in their classrooms. I marked my calendar to be in the classrooms for about two hours each day. I assured the teachers that my visits would deal just with our focus on reading instruction and that I would tell them precisely what I would be looking for and give them examples and a written list of what I expected us to work toward cooperatively as a faculty.

UNEXPECTED CHALLENGES

On the following Monday, excited that I finally will be able to start getting into each classroom over the next few weeks, I receive a phone call from my supervisor informing me of a mandatory Red Cross meeting taking place that very day. I explain to my supervisor that the teachers are expecting me in the classrooms and ask if I may go to a later meeting. He reminds me that I had put off the last three presentations and says I must go today. So I drive to the meeting.

As I enter the large room, the Red Cross speaker begins: "Welcome. I know you are excited to be here! We are thrilled to meet the pillars of our community and *you*, our Red Cross *volunteers*! [*What, I'm a Red Cross volunteer?*] I know you realize that near the Atlantic Ocean we have disaster shelters in our schools during hurricane season. You are in charge of these shelters! [*Oh, please God, no!*] Today, in this short four hours, we will give you the requirements set down by the American Red Cross. These guidelines have been approved by your superintendent and the School Board."

The presentation goes on: "We would appreciate your *undivided* attention at this meeting. This is serious business. You may be responsible for saving *lives* in our community. You are *completely* in charge of the shelter at your school. Should any disaster arise, we will contact you immediately. We will maintain the control center here and give you assistance through a CB operator. We normally have about four hurricane warnings yearly with potential for more.

"Here is the procedure: We first contact you to open the shelter. Our priority is for you to place our radio operator in your office. Then call in your custodians and lunchroom manager. Do an inventory of food and decide how many people you can feed and sleep. Contact us with that number within two hours. We never send more then 200–400 displaced people to one school, if possible. Questions so far?'"

I am furiously writing notes. *You have got to be kidding! I am supposed to be in charge of all this? Give me a break!* I start taking deep breaths to calm myself and wonder how I can add this to my list of jobs to do.

He continues: "People in the potential danger areas will be advised via television/radio to come to your school. Their evacuation will take place ten to twelve hours before the storm is predicted to hit. They will bring their own blankets, personal items, and prescriptions. That is *all* they are allowed to bring. Some will try to bring their pets. *You must not allow any pets!* Red Cross strictly prohibits any pets on the premises. Just people. This is a most important rule."

The meeting goes on and on, with speeches, videotapes of actual shelters, guidelines, and reminders of rules. The speaker tells us, "The Red Cross will reimburse the school system for supplies used during the disaster." No moneys will be allocated to lunchroom staff to cook meals, custodians to set up the shelter, or the principal. By the time the meeting is over, I am convinced that being a *warden* during this hurricane season is another very important—*and completely unexpected*—responsibility as principal. Back at the office we make a big red file folder labeled "Red Cross Instructions" for ready access to the material when needed.

That evening I remain several hours at school, reading important letters, making notes to myself, answering teacher requests, and calling parents. Before I leave, I list my priorities for the next few days. Once again my main priority is visiting classrooms. I never expected that many weeks would pass before I could get to my coaching of the teachers. I console myself that my groundwork over the summer for the classroom assignment of students, my brief drop-in visits to classrooms, and my orientation of the faculty about my instruction priorities have already been done. At least I know that the climate for good instruction has been established.

OFFSETTING STRESS ABOUT CLASSROOM VISITS

Teachers know that classroom visits by the principal are required by the state. But we talk about this once again at our faculty meeting on Tuesday. I explain my focus and give them written guidelines for my visits:

1. I will wear a large button that says "Just Visiting." The teacher and the children are to keep working, so that instruction will not be interrupted. This is an informational visit, and you will not be evaluated. I will be making written comments to you but only on the positive things I see in your classroom. I will leave my notes on your desk when I leave.

2. I will look at the general appearance of the classroom. This includes cleanliness and attractive bulletin boards. It would be an asset if bulletin boards include examples of children's work and motivational materials geared to the children's level, for example, pictures of what is being studied in science, art contributions of children, or creative writing, and so on.

3. I will only come during language arts time, as reflected on your lesson plans. If I enter the classroom as the children are working independently, then I will take note of what they are doing. I will especially

check to see if any children are *stuck* and do not understand an assignment. To be effective, children's seat work assignments should be matched to their level, allowing them to maintain a minimum of 85 percent mastery. Independent seat work should only be practice work for mastering skills and concepts the child has already obtained from the teacher's direct instruction, cooperative learning, or peer teaching.

4. If I see a child off task, then I will quietly question the child and help. This will give me a cursory view of whether the child is being successful. (A child's self-confidence as a learner is directly related to achievement. Being able to complete assignments effectively and with assurance is especially important for building self-esteem.)

5. With effective instruction, classrooms are rarely totally quiet. According to research, children teaching children is an effective way for them to learn. I welcome effective interaction between teachers and children as well as children and other children. (The only exception to this is when a teacher is directly teaching the class. All children must be quiet and listen.)

6. Before I come for any evaluations, I will be glad to do demonstration teaching in reading or language arts.

MY FIRST DEMONSTRATION LESSON

My first official classroom demonstration lesson is in creative writing in the fifth grade. Elaine is a first-year teacher who requests that I help motivate her children to want to write. So I demonstrate creative writing instruction. After perusing the teachers' edition in language arts, I go to the classroom. Because the teacher has requested a motivational lesson, I let the children brainstorm ideas for the writing subject. They pick favorite television shows as a topic.

After listing several favorite programs, the children narrow the choices down to two: *Even Stevens* from Walt Disney and *Law and Order*. We vote on which show will be the topic of our creative writing. *Law and Order* is the winner. We come up with facts about the show, episodes they remember, and impressions they have. Then we write adjectives and nouns on the chalkboard that best characterize the show. As the children raise their hands and contribute, I put their words on the chalkboard. I explain that each person will write a story based on *Law and Order*.

As we brainstorm, we talk about how to make complete sentences and review rules about main ideas and paragraphs. Because we leave the brainstormed words and phrases on the chalkboard, the children who are slower can draw on the ideas and correct spellings as they write their stories.

As they begin to complete their fifteen- to twenty-minute writing lesson, the teacher and I circulate. A few children are very slow in writing, and I sit down with some to encourage them. Individually, we advise them on indenting, paragraph alignment, and other technical aspects of writing. The teacher and I have stressed that creativity is an individual matter and that children are creative and talented in many different ways. We encourage these different perspectives as we work with the children individually.

Because writing is stressed in every grade from kindergarten through fifth, the children have good technical skills in fifth grade. But there are many different ability levels. Elaine and I identify some serious deficiencies. As I leave the room, we make a follow-up appointment for after school.

That afternoon, as Elaine comes into the office, she is full of appreciation: "You know, Dr. Lawrence, the children really love to have the principal come in and teach them. They feel so important! I am so glad you are taking this time. You helped remind me that making the lesson relevant to their lives makes a big difference in their interest in trying to write."

I reply, "Thank you. I enjoyed teaching them. I was tickled when they were testing me to see if they could use some marginal adjectives about *Law and Order*. When Jarvis used the word *pimp*, I knew we were heading in the wrong direction. They do love to test us, don't they?

"Elaine, you do have your work cut out for you with the wide spread of writing abilities. You know Michelle is very sophisticated in her writing, and then I see Jarvis, who is afraid to use his imagination at all. Most of the children still need practice to master some of the technical aspects of writing. How did you experience the lesson?"

"Well, I can tell that I have a lot of work to do to iron out special problems with several children. But I'm excited about the prospect of expanding stories relevant to their lives. I hope I can bring them a long way in trusting themselves about being creative and being more willing to take risks."

"I'd like for you to keep me posted. Why don't you keep these stories, and then let's compare their progress in another two or three months? When you compare the two sets of work with them, I am sure they will be surprised at how much they have learned."

We talked about effectively managing the skill-level differences in her classroom. She told me about the particular developmental characteristics of fifth graders and her plans for dealing with them. Because she was a new teacher, I offered her the opportunity to visit a fifth grade teacher in another school. The other teacher was especially talented in creative writing, managing differences with cooperative learning strategies, and peer tutoring. Elaine was delighted, and I gave the secretary instructions to make the arrangements.

As she left my office, she said that she felt we were now partners for instruction in her classroom. I was thrilled when she said this. I was getting to be an instructional principal! I hoped I could develop this kind of relationship with many of my teachers.

VISITING CLASSROOMS DURING
READING INSTRUCTION

I believe that the schoolwide improvements we saw in all academic measures directly stemmed from my close supervision of reading instruction, teacher by teacher. If you are a principal or planning to be one, then you must be thinking at this point, "Oh, my word, on top of everything else I have to do, I have to be a coach of reading instruction too?"

Well, yes, to some degree if you want to try the system that was successful for us. This does not mean that you have to take a course. To begin you can follow the guidelines that worked well for me when observing reading instruction. These simple but important guidelines include the following:

1. When the teacher is meeting with a reading group, watch to see that each child, individually, is able to read back orally to the teacher, without missing many words. If a child reading to the teacher stumbles repeatedly or reads haltingly with several errors, then the reading material is not on the correct *instructional* level. This means that the

teacher has not correctly assessed the child's level of instruction and needs to reassess that child. Make a note to the teacher.

2. In the primary grades, reading instruction must take place every day—with the teacher using the teacher's manual for each reading group. I told my teachers that if they conscientiously taught twenty-five to thirty minutes of progressive reading instruction to every reading group four days a week, they could take the fifth day off and work on other activities. I would not visit any classrooms for any kind of coaching or evaluations on Fridays. As a first grade teacher of many years, I successfully used this practice and found that Friday was my day to regroup, pull materials out for the next week, and make plans. The class and I took a needed break from intense instruction and did other activities.

3. After visiting a teacher during reading, always leave a note about positive things that happened during the visit.

4. Set up a follow-up conference with all the teachers you visit to give feedback and get their view of what you observed.

5. Because the primary concern is reading, visit only during language arts instruction for the first year.

TEACHER GUIDELINES FOR READING INSTRUCTION

Before I visited any teachers to observe reading lessons, I gave them all a sheet of guidelines I would use in my observations. We talked in faculty meetings several times about this, as I wanted them to understand the practical applications of these research-based guidelines. I wanted the teachers to know that these are markers of effective instruction:

1. Reading instruction will be given in small groups—typically seven to ten children each—reading quietly with the teacher. Having all the children in the class reading together out loud is not acceptable; it does not allow the teacher to detect the specific skill needs and problems of an individual child.

2. Children should be reading individually to the teacher so that the teacher can determine, after teaching the new words and concepts,

that each child is absorbing what is necessary each day. The whole reading process is broken down sequentially in the teacher's edition, and one complete story should take a minimum of four days. Many, many teachers think that just reading the story and quickly going over the words are enough. This is absolutely not true, and throughout my teaching career I tested this over and over.

3. Using the teacher's edition is essential. Even though a teacher has taught the same reading series for many years, he or she will need the suggestions in the manual for setting the climate of the story, introducing vocabulary words with specific sentences the children can understand, and so on. The reading charts in the teacher's manual are also needed to give the children a visual scheme of the words and sentences being used.

4. In their reading groups, children should be working and reading on an instructional level that is correct for them, that is, they should struggle occasionally with some new words but be able, with the teacher's help, to decode them. The teacher moves them along slowly but surely, by reemphasizing concepts as they read.

5. While the teacher is working with one reading group, the rest of the students must be doing some kind of constructive seat work during the entire time. The seat work needs to be selected carefully to engage and hold the children's attention. It needs to be work that they can do independently, without the teacher's guidance. The children must be taught that reading group time is a sacred time and that children who are not in the reading group absolutely cannot interrupt the teacher for any reason except a true emergency. It takes about two weeks to train the children to work within the plan.

I told the teachers I would be helping them select good seat work materials and showing them how to set up small heterogeneous groups in seat work centers. We also started a materials center for all the teachers. This room was devoted to well-tested games and manipulative learning materials that could be used by the children for their seat work. This room was organized so the teachers could easily pick out materials on the correct instructional level of the children.

MY FIRST READING GROUP
DEMONSTRATION LESSON

Following these meetings I arranged to go to a first grade teacher's classroom for a demonstration of reading instruction, which she had requested. I am very excited about it. The only stipulation I have for Mrs. Watson is that I teach the group of her children with the least reading ability. I figure that if she can see how I teach them, then she will be able to follow the plan more easily with the more advanced children.

About three weeks prior to coming to the classroom for the reading demonstration lesson, I work with Mrs. Watson on how to set up effective seat work centers in the classroom. These centers are for practice work only, usually using manipulative, self-correcting materials from the central manipulative room, which also includes the books and materials for the reading series. Teaching the children the system of using centers is a somewhat arduous task. The process is covered in a small book entitled *The Practice Centers Approach to Seat-Work: A Handbook,* by Lawrence, Lawrence, and Galloway (1989).

As I enter the classroom, I tell the children how I want to get to know each child in our school and that I appreciate their teacher letting me borrow them as my children to teach for four days. I explain that I will be coming Monday through Thursday for thirty minutes to work in the classroom with one reading group (I use the four days to show Mrs. Watson the complete cycle of completing one story).

That first morning, with my reading group, I set the scene for the story using dialogue from the teacher's edition. The children are well behaved and excited about having the principal teach them. The teacher's edition is very easy to follow in going over particular skills, including the chart pages, workbook pages, and foundation questions to get the children comfortable with trying to read the story.

The children's names are Betsy, John, D. J., Janie, Daniel, Joe, and Tony. Seven children are in this reading group. This is good. I have cautioned the teachers in first grade that over ten children in one group may be too many to allow adequate time to detect problems in understanding, the fear of trying to read, and comprehension (being able to figure out a word using sounds, context clues, or the pictures in the story).

I begin: "Today we get to start a great new story about a mother polar bear and a baby polar bear! Is there anyone (raise your hand) who can tell me how a polar bear is different from just any bear? You can look at the picture on the front of the story in your book. Okay, Janie, how is the polar bear different?"

Janie replies, "It's white."

"Janie, that is exactly correct," I tell her, "but instead of saying, 'It's white,' could you make a whole sentence for me?"

Janie corrects herself and says, "The polar bear is white."

"Wonderful," I say. "Now Janie is really getting sophisticated in making complete sentences." (Using big words impresses the children, and I explain what *sophisticated* means.)

"Is there anything else you can tell me about the picture of the polar bear?" D. J. raises his hand: "The polar bears like the snow and the cold water."

"D. J. that is excellent, and what a good long, complete sentence. Good for you!

"I have to tell you all how I am loving teaching this reading group. You are sitting so quietly, sitting up straight [five bodies immediately straighten their backs and look at me expectantly]; I am so pleased with all of you."

Just looking at the pictures, talking about bear experiences, telling reactions, and fostering interest in what this story may be about take the entire thirty minutes. During this time I make sure that every child gets to answer a question correctly, is given praise, and looks forward to the next day.

That afternoon I go over the lesson with the teacher and explain exactly what I did and where I am heading with the instruction. On Tuesday, we learn the few new vocabulary words—such as the word *tame*—that are introduced in the story. We learn the words by practicing from a chart—with questions from me.

"Boys and girls, this word is the opposite of *wild* and rhymes with *came*. Can you guess what the word is? *The little dog is very _____.*" This is the pattern for introducing the five new vocabulary words.

By the end of all four lessons, we have read the story. Every child has answered comprehension questions for me separately, after they have read quietly in the group to themselves. I have observed all the children long enough to tell if they are on the correct instructional level and are moving at an adequate pace.

Mrs. Watson has been with me for the four reading sessions with this group, so she has seen the definite pattern for teaching reading, which I know to be effective. She has seen specifically how I tell exactly where each child is in the reading process.

She has seen the time and patience needed in waiting for a child to answer a specific question, even though all others have to sit quietly and listen. The teacher has to know exactly what stumbling blocks each child is experiencing; otherwise, the child reaches a frustration level, with gaps in understanding, and will require extra help. Reading on the frustration level only leads the child to hate reading.

I have answered every question she has had about the reading group. One particular question that is frequently asked is: "Can't the children just read the story out loud in unison instead of quietly reading each page to themselves?"

My answer to this is a very emphatic, *"No!"* When children read in unison, the teacher is unable to spot a child's particular reading problem. Many times children can read words without comprehending what they mean. Teaching for comprehension is one of the most difficult aspects of the reading process. When children read out loud together there is no way a teacher can check for individual comprehension.

There is another major point against just reading the story together and going through it quickly. Teachers must let the children read a page quietly to themselves. By giving all the children in the group a comprehension question before having them read one page to themselves, the teacher can then watch the children. As the children read quietly, the teacher can observe who seems to really be reading the sentences and words, for most children read moving their lips. Then when the teacher asks a child a comprehension question, he or she can tell if the child understands what is being read.

That afternoon Mrs. Watson comes in for a visit about the lesson. We go over what impressions she has about the way I taught reading. We also discuss her anxiety about being sure the children are reading at their correct level and ideas for how she can find more time during the day to teach reading. I assure Mrs. Watson that reading is the most important subject she teaches in first grade. I also tell her not to worry about how much material she covers but, rather, about how thoroughly she covers the materials as she goes along. When she leaves the office, she tells me that she is much more aware of what I expect now. She also appreciates the time I spent teaching in her classroom.

A VERY UNPLEASANT CLASSROOM VISIT

Mrs. Monroe was one of the teachers who did not invite me to visit her class-room. She was one of the last teachers I visited. Although I had asked Mrs. Monroe several times for her choice of when she would like to have me come to her room, she had never responded. Finally, I advised her that I would be in during her language arts time the following afternoon.

As I enter Mrs. Monroe's classroom the following week I am very dismayed to see the children copying page after page from the chalkboard, with no apparent teaching on Mrs. Monroe's part. This is a classroom of twelve special needs children, who scored very low on the aptitude tests. The work on the chalkboard does not take into account different levels, and the children are just copying it. Because this is merely a first informational visit and I promised to stay only a few minutes, I decide that perhaps she has not understood some of the directions we have discussed. I tell her that I will be back the next day to observe her language arts instruction.

When I return the next day, during language arts period, all the children are working diligently, copying from the chalkboard. As I read what they are copying, I see that the assignment is taken from pages out of a social studies book.

I walk over to the teacher, who has been teaching the special needs class for the past seventeen years at Prescott, and whisper, "Mrs. Monroe, why have your children been copying from the chalkboard the last two times I have been in to observe? Would you tell me when is a good time to see you teaching the children in small groups or individually?"

Mrs. Monroe says to me very condescendingly, "Dr. Lawrence, these children cannot learn. They are just barely trainable. They can copy from the board, and I hope they pick up something from what they are copying. But if I don't keep them busy every minute of every day, copying, then they will develop discipline problems."

I say: "Mrs. Monroe, I would like to have a conference with you this afternoon." She agrees, and I leave the classroom.

When she comes into my office that afternoon, she is very calm, reserved, and sure of herself. After all the faculty meetings, discussion of research, help I have offered on correct instructional levels, and so forth, I am furious and perplexed at her attitude. These children are not being given adequate instruction. Thankfully, in my job as curriculum resource teacher, I had much experience doing demonstration teaching for classes of this type. When one exceptional student educator became ill, I took over the class for a total of six weeks. I know specifically that all children can learn. The only real adjustment you have to make for children of limited intelligence is to work a lot on developing a positive self-image-as-learner and to get each child on the correct instructional level. I had checked the diagnostic screening of Mrs. Monroe's children, and even though they were low in terms of ability, they were educable, not merely trainable. Given the right amount of time and help, they were capable of learning.

"Mrs. Monroe, I have taught mentally handicapped children. Teaching children with limited intelligence means teaching them very, very slowly, checking to see that they learn each concept to mastery before trying a new concept, and building one educational block at a time.

"I am very disturbed that you think they can't learn but can merely copy from the board. You have had some of these children, who are in fifth grade, since first grade. I need to help you with diversifying their instruction."

"No, Dr. Lawrence, you do not. I have been teaching for thirty-seven years and have spent the last seventeen years teaching these handicapped children. There is just so much you can do with them. Mainly, I just have to keep them busy. I have never had a complaint about my teaching. I want you to know you are a young principal, and I feel that you don't know what you are doing. Administrators of this new generation think they know everything. If you don't leave me alone, I will just resign."

I reply: "Mrs. Monroe, I am not going to leave you or your children alone. I am heartsick that your children are not being taught as individuals. The reason you have twelve children in your class is to give you much more time to work with the children individually, to give them a lot of extra help on their level. I will be coming into your classroom to check on reading instruction levels, and I will be helping you with your instruction."

"Dr. Lawrence, I have an ESE [Exceptional Student Education] supervisor at the district level who comes and gives me help if I need it. I don't need or want your help."

I am just speechless that this older woman is so resentful of my visiting her classroom and that she is furious with me for even suggesting that she may need help. I tell her that I will be coming into her classroom the next day to begin assessing the specific reading levels of her children.

Mrs. Monroe leaves the office telling me that she will be calling the teachers' union and her supervisor and that she will file a grievance against me for interfering with her work. She cites the fact that she has been doing this same instruction for seventeen years without any problems.

That afternoon I check into her professional file for information on her background. Her teacher evaluations, sure enough, are satisfactory. She has even received positive statements about her control of her children. I am still determined to go into the room and to work with each child, find out their levels in reading, and be sure that they are getting adequate reading instruction.

The following morning, before I had time to get into any of the classrooms, I received a call from the president of the teachers' union. I knew her well as a former fellow teacher and know she was an excellent teacher with high standards.

I told her exactly what I observed during my visits to Mrs. Monroe's classroom. I also told her of my plan to work with the children and that I would inform her of the outcome. She warned that I might be stirring up trouble for myself by doing this. I told her that I would call my supervisor at the district level to get approval of my plan.

When I called my supervisor and told him the situation, he congratulated me on attacking the problem. He told me specifically what I could and could not do about helping Mrs. Monroe. He advised me that I was completely within my rights as a principal in ensuring that the children were receiving proper instruction.

Within the week, I had worked with each of the twelve children in this special class to identify reading levels. The children were on several levels. We had materials in the school appropriate for each level, and I pulled them together and gave them, labeled for each child, to Mrs. Monroe. Mrs. Monroe refused to work with me, and I gave her a very poor evaluation—listing dates, times, and conversations surrounding her refusal to follow instructions. At the end of the year, she chose to resign.

By the end of my first year as principal, Mrs. Monroe became very vocal in telling everyone on my staff how I had singled her out for intimidation for no reason. As a professional, a principal is *never* allowed to discuss a teacher's problem with anyone except an administrative assistant or supervisor. I was able to respond with sound reasoning when contacted by the union president.

Most elementary schools do not have an assistant principal or a full-time administrative assistant. In these cases the principal has no one with whom to share these kinds of problems. The position of elementary school principal is lonely and isolated most of the time. I could not respond to any rumors or questions to justify my actions with Mrs. Monroe. I just hoped that I had enough credibility with the faculty to withstand this minor assault.

REFLECTING ON MY FIRST YEAR AS PRINCIPAL

Grades on Report Cards

Throughout the school year, theoretically, children had been working on their own individual instructional level in reading. I read each child's report card, every nine weeks, before they were distributed to the parents. This allowed me to see teachers' written comments, check their grammar, and watch for children who were getting low grades in reading (and any other subject).

The district grading system for report cards was as follows: A: superior (100–94); B: above average (93–87); C: average (86–79); D: below average (78–75); and F: failing (74 and below). However, we graded the children on their performance *at their instructional level* in reading rather than for their grade level. We used the system I had negotiated at the school where I taught first grade almost twenty years earlier. For performance in reading, we gave each child a two-part grade. The letter part of the grade (A, B, C, D) was for the child's success at his or her correct instruction level. The second part of the grade was a number indicating the grade level at which the child was reading. So, for example, a third grader's reading grade of B/2 meant that he or she was reading at second grade level and making above-average progress.

The faculty and I decided to reserve *A* grades only for children who were reading grade-level material. When a grade of A is given, we wanted it to mean that the child was ready to move to the next grade level of reading work.

Using the "F" Letter at Our School

I viewed a grade of *failure* or *F* on a report card as a possible failure on our part to provide adequately for the child's learning needs. If a child was recommended to be retained, I would only okay this under very specific circumstances. During the school year, the teachers knew that a failing grade was an indicator to me that the teacher and I needed a conference.

Every nine weeks, teachers who were giving an F in any subject came and talked with me. I wanted to know specifically what was happening. If the grade was caused by the child's lack of effort or anything the child had failed to do that could have been done, I had no problem with the failure. Many times, however, we talked out specific strategies for improving the instruction and especially the correct instructional level in reading.

I specifically remember one child named Marcus who was passed to fifth grade against the wishes of his teacher. I read his cumulative folder, and the aptitude scores showed that he had above-average ability but had always had bad grades. The following year I decided to watch Marcus and check on his progress. I sat in his class a couple of times a week for a while and watched him. I spoke with him several times on a casual basis in the lunchroom or around the campus, trying to figure out why this child, with such good ability, was failing over and over. He was not a discipline problem at all, and his scores on district and state tests were average.

I asked our district gifted supervisor to come out and talk with me about Marcus. She was a friend of mine, and I asked her to do this as a favor. I told her that I just had a hunch that Marcus was a gifted child, from great hardworking African American parents, who for some reason was falling through the cracks in the regular classroom.

Jeri looked over his cumulative folder and was very intrigued. She was an extremely able supervisor of the gifted and loved to bring as many marginal children into the gifted program as could meet certain criteria. One criterion had to do with aptitude scores versus performance in the classroom, and another concerned scores in the classroom versus scores on district and state testing. So there was a clause in her program that allowed her discretion in pulling in particular children.

Thus Marcus was given a little extra leeway and was entered into the program about the middle of October. This was a full-time program. Within four months, Marcus was working very hard to catch up with the other children and never had to be dropped from the gifted program.

Just recently, nine years later, Jeri sent me a picture of Marcus on the front page of the local newspaper. Marcus had won a full scholarship in music to a very prestigious university. In the article, he was asked who had the most influence on his educational success. Marcus said: "My elementary principal and the supervisor of the gifted programs when I was in fifth grade." Needless to say, Jeri and I were and are thrilled. These are the victories teachers cherish. This is what correct instructional level and individual attention are all about.

The End of the School Year

For the bulk of the first school year, I spent an average of four hours a week in the classrooms. All the visits were done during language arts and reading instruction time. I worked with the teachers on correct instructional level, keeping tabs on the children's reading levels. At the end of the year I required teachers to give to me a card on each child, with their current reading level, gender, special learning problems, and any disciplinary problems. The cards were to help me plan the next year and place the children in reading groups for the fall semester.

The more time I spent in the classrooms, the more I became aware that I had several teachers who needed major help in instruction. I also had many more teachers who were clearly outstanding and even heroic in their educational efforts.

When I made a list at the end of the year of my instructional staff, I found that out of thirty-four teachers I had twenty good to excellent educators, some of whom I discuss in chapter 6. I had five marginally effective teachers who needed help but, with enough instruction, could become solid educators. I clearly had seven incompetent teachers, which is an unheard-of amount in a school the size of Prescott, and they all were on tenure (continuing contract). I needed personally to give them special detailed help, to do demonstration teaching, and to give them every available chance to improve. That is part of the due process required before dismissal action can be initiated.

Many marginal and incompetent teachers, when recognizing that they are going to be carefully scrutinized by the principal, will try to transfer to another school. Some principals, when asked about a teacher on the transfer list, will give the marginal or incompetent teacher a slightly higher rating than deserved. I feel that the transferring of any teacher who is incompetent, or who might be incompetent, is unprofessional. These teachers were my teachers and needed to be helped in becoming good educators or needed to get out of the field of education, not just be swapped from one school to another.

With the marginal and incompetent teachers in mind, I scheduled an appointment with the superintendent, took him a chart of these teachers, and showed him the particulars on the teachers who needed major help. I asked him for help, explaining that Prescott had clearly been "dumped on" by district transfers over the years. This often happens with less affluent schools because the parents are not as literate or assertive and are not as likely to create problems. I showed him documented proof of the transfers over the years. I truly believe that this happens in all districts throughout our country.

I asked that he allow Betsy, my administrative assistant, who was then teaching first grade, to become a full-time assistant, and he agreed. By having Betsy as a full-time assistant, I knew I could then make more classroom visits every day. Betsy and I would share administrative duties. He agreed.

Meeting with the Teachers at the End of the First Year

At the end of the year, I met with each of the teachers individually. We discussed pluses and minuses of the school year and our work on instruction. Not surprisingly, I found that some of my teachers were not accustomed to being monitored in the classrooms. One particular excellent fourth grade teacher remarked to me, "A few of the teachers just don't understand you. They are not used to the principal being so involved with their teaching. I like to have you come in and support me with instruction, but many of the teachers do not. They feel they have been instructing successfully for years without the principal being involved and don't feel the need of close supervision."

Teachers consider having autonomy in the classroom as one of the major perks of the profession. Teachers consider themselves professionals who deserve the trust of the administration to do their jobs well. I truly believe this. I tried my best the first year to be as nonthreatening as possible. But few teachers expect the principal to be knowledgeable about instruction or to have time to do instruction in the classrooms. When they close the door in the mornings, their classroom is their haven. As a classroom teacher for seventeen years, I remember how much I enjoyed being trusted and being left alone.

But during the past ten to fifteen years, the pattern has changed. Principals are expected to visit classrooms. A lot of time and money have been spent on developing observation and evaluative instruments for the principal, with very specific guidelines. In the hands of principals without an instructional background, the instruments can be used with a narrow view of instruction—with which the teachers disagree.

Principals of elementary education who know instruction are able to bring appropriate interpretations to items on these instruments in K–5 situations. For instance, when observing *high-level questioning skills* on an evaluative instrument, obviously the kindergarten and first grade teachers are evaluated with different criteria than the upper grade–level teachers. Children in kindergarten and the first grade are still in the *concrete operational stage,* which means that higher-order questioning is mostly above their frame of reference. The teachers of primary children can help them to see concrete consequences and meanings but not to do abstract reasoning.

With all the time and money spent on developing evaluative instruments, I am required to evaluate responsibly, just as I am thoroughly evaluated myself. That is the expectation for today's schools.

Some principals only do a cursory evaluation of teachers they regard as excellent, just marking them excellent in every category as a kind of token of appreciation. My older faculty, with an average time at Prescott of twenty-two years, had begun their careers when the old style of autonomy was in vogue, and they were given more general evaluations. When the new observation instruments were mandated, they became used to having more evaluations, more often, but they did not have a principal who knew more about instruction than they did.

All the work I did the first year did break some barriers about helping the teachers. I especially remember comments of appreciation after I helped teachers with their classrooms. They never expected so much help. When I helped a fifth grade teacher with his lesson plans he said to me, "You are the first principal in twenty-seven years who ever sat down with me and helped me with an instructional problem. This help with lesson plans is just amazing and so simple. The process is so much easier than I had anticipated, and it makes sense."

Whatever they felt about my assistance, though, I knew that I was the boss and had the final say on their evaluations. So, quite naturally, they all were a little intimidated, even my excellent teachers, and some naturally viewed me with suspicion.

So during my year-end meeting with each teacher, I clearly explained my plans for the coming year. I praised them all for their positive contributions and accomplishments. For the marginal teachers specifically, I went over what I had seen about their instruction, where they were having difficulty, how I would continue to help them, and what I expected in the new school year.

Over the first year, I had spent time with those teachers who I believed needed major help. Some classroom teachers had received specific demonstration teaching by me in their classrooms, to give them every possible advantage. In a few cases, I got Betsy a substitute for her classroom whom she trusted and made her administrator on those days. Then I was able to take over a classroom for a period of one week, doing the teaching, grading of papers, and planning. In this way, I felt that the teachers could see what was possible with their own children. I gave them ample time and attention to know what I expected of them. I realized that they did not have my same way of teaching, but I knew that I had shown them many ideas for improvement.

Resignations and Transfers

I was not surprised that, over the summer, one of the teachers whom I considered incompetent resigned. The Educable Mentally Handicapped (EMH) teacher, Mrs. Monroe, who had her children copy from the chalkboard, decided to retire after thirty-seven years. I was very thankful for her resignation because she had grudgingly done only a small portion of her improvement plan.

Too many times, in public education, marginal or poor teachers are given to these special classrooms because they cannot handle either instruction or discipline in regular classrooms. Because the EMH classrooms typically have nine to fourteen students, the principal hopes that the teacher will be able to handle a smaller number. Some principals believe, mistakenly, that this class would be easier to teach. The opposite is true. Handicapped children actually require teachers to have more education and skill than regular classroom teachers. They must have exceptional knowledge of the instructional process because they have so many different kinds of problems, including some children with emotional handicaps. These children are the very ones who may never make it in our society without almost one-on-one instruction. With the extra help, most of them, clearly, can become functional individuals with productive lives.

Another resignation, from Mrs. Ellis, the learning disability (LD) resource teacher, was a blessing to me and the faculty. Even though she was a resource teacher, I found that she had very little knowledge of reading instruction and, I suspected, spent some of her day just visiting teachers who were on break in the lounge.

I will never forget one day that Betsy and I had a strange encounter as we went into my small office to talk about a problem with the lunchroom staff. My office was connected to the main office by a short hallway, with a door on each end of the hall. Because of the hallway into the main office, which I thought was enough of a buffer to give privacy, I just opened my door and pushed it into the wall behind it. As we talked somehow I had an uneasy feeling that another person was in the room with us. I went over to the door, pulled it back from the wall, and found Mrs. Ellis squashed behind it.

"Mrs. Ellis, what in the world are you doing behind the door?"

Mrs. Ellis replied, "Well, I was just in your office and kind of got behind the door because I didn't want you to know I was in your office."

"Why would you be worried about being in my office? You know everyone is allowed in my office, while I'm not using it, to use the phone or whatever." I was truly taken aback to find her hiding behind the door. Betsy and I had been talking for a full five minutes.

She looked very embarrassed, said she did not want to interrupt our conversation, and exited as gracefully as she could. After she left, Betsy told me that Mrs. Ellis loved to find out gossip about the principal, secretaries, teachers, and staff and seemed to spend a major part of her day just visiting teachers on break or anywhere she could catch anyone. Her purpose was just to gossip and find out something that others may not know. Betsy thought Mrs. Ellis believed that other teachers would hold her in high regard for this. I was astonished.

Suddenly I realized that my work with Mrs. Ellis that year—getting her into the classrooms, working out her time schedule, and getting her more organized—had been a more complex task for her than I realized. She could not keep her old routine and still do the things I told her were her jobs to do.

Luckily, I knew of a former, masterful LD resource teacher returning from leave who knew this job well, had taught primary grade reading for years, and was a hard worker. She would take a big load off my shoulders, that of screening children and helping teachers with reading. So I called her immediately and got her to agree to come to Prescott.

During the same summer, two of my clearly marginal teachers applied for transfers to another school. Transferring was a standard practice in our district for many reasons, such as getting closer to home, wanting to try another school, or just having a personality problem with the principal or staff.

When a teacher requests to be transferred, usually the principal of the new school will call the principal who has worked with that teacher for information about him or her. The principal needs to know that the teacher is not hiring a problem. I think it is only professional to tell the principal the absolute truth. Although I would have loved for these teachers to leave, I could not recommend them to teach children at another school. On the other hand, if there is a personality conflict with me and the teachers have good ability, then I have no reservations about them going where they will be more comfortable.

So my second year would be starting with the same faculty, minus one teacher I was glad to see gone, plus an excellent curriculum resource teacher, an excellent LD resource teacher, and someone to take Betsy's first grade class. Once again, the children were placed by stratified random assignment, giving each teacher three reading levels. That summer we purchased reading materials for the year based on these reading ability levels.

5

RAMIFICATIONS
OF POVERTY

After the first three to four months of school, the weather began to turn cool. Increasingly, I began to hear from the teachers about children coming to school chilled without adequate clothing.

One morning Mrs. Jones, an excellent kindergarten teacher, brought Justin into the office. She was frustrated and very upset. She left Justin in the outer office with the secretary and said to me, "Dr. Lawrence, I really need help with Justin. The children are refusing to sit by him because he smells so bad and is so dirty."

I brought him into the office alone with me. He did indeed have a pronounced odor and filthy clothes. I looked at his feet and saw that his shoes were those of an adult male. They were tied around his feet with large shoelaces to hold them on. He really looked pitiful as he shuffled over to my desk. "Justin, are those too big for you?"

He answered: "No, they are okay. My dad gave me some old ones of his. My foot doesn't fit into mine anymore. But my dad said I could wear these."

"Justin, would you sit in my conference room and draw or play with this puzzle? I will be back in just a minute."

"Okay," he said, "I love to draw boats, and I can work puzzles, too."

I went and found Betsy to ask her about Justin. She told me that he was the second of five children: "The father is in prison. The mother works two jobs, one during the day and one at night. The oldest is Sandra, seven, and she babysits the other four, including one about two years old. The grandmother keeps the two younger ones during the day, but she also works at night. The mother and grandmother qualify for welfare, but both refuse to take it. They actually would have more money if they did take welfare, but when I spoke with them, they said that they were too proud to take welfare."

That afternoon I kept Justin and Sandra with me until about 5:00 PM and then drove them to their grandmother's house. I met the grandmother and the younger children. Sandra had shown me the way to their house. I was amazed and utterly shocked to find dirt floors.

Sandra ushered me in and said, "My mom doesn't get home until after we go to bed, but we see her in the morning before we leave for school. She stays home all day with us on Sundays, and that's when we have a great time!" Sandra was one of the prettiest girls I had ever seen, with a very mature and nurturing manner with the children. They followed her directions about putting up their books, and I could tell that all the children really cared for each other.

The dirt floors were swept clean and neat. I was appalled to find that there was no apparent heat in the house. When I asked Sandra about supper for the children, she said, "We don't eat supper at night. We eat our meals at school. We have breakfast and lunch."

I found not one bit of food in the house anywhere, not even a box of crackers or a can of soup. The children did not seem concerned. Two turned on a small TV, and two went to play in the front yard.

I left Sandra and told her that I would be right back. I went to a phone and called our social worker at home. I told her where I had just been and said, "Louise, I am dying here. These five children have no food for tonight and say they don't eat supper! Did you know about them?"

"I knew that Sandra keeps all the children at night, but I didn't know they have no food. Do you want me to go get them some groceries?"

"Please, and I will reimburse you when you get here. Just buy enough staples like milk, bread, peanut butter, some fruit, and cereal to get them by until we can find some way to help. I am going to take a load of clothes home with me tonight so they can have clean clothes tomorrow. They don't have a washing machine or hot water, I already checked."

Louise agreed to go to the store, buy some groceries for me, and feed them that night. The next day she came to me with $50.00 in cash. She said, "Dr. Lawrence, I got this money from a drug dealer painting his house last night after you called. I climbed up that ladder, and I said, 'I know you are dealing drugs and have extra money. I remember you as a student in Prescott. We have children that are hungry tonight, and I need money. Now you just come on down here and give me some money for these children. You can just pay back some of the drug money you get from some of the parents!'" Then she very proudly told me that he gave her $74.00 without even a grumble.

I was astounded (and tickled) that this sixty-year-old matronly woman had climbed a ladder and demanded money from this drug dealer. She did not seem to be intimidated at all and said that she knew most of the drug dealers when they were young students and was not afraid of them. I told her that we would need to discuss this tactic at length later but that I had an emergency faculty meeting scheduled now to talk about poverty issues.

THE FACULTY AND PTA FIND SOLUTIONS

In the faculty meeting, as I told the story of the night before, I did not see many teachers surprised. The discussion turned up a variety of ways that poverty was interfering with our students' learning. Some children were coming to school hungry in the mornings from not having an evening meal, and some came without adequate clothing. Others had clothing so dirty and such body odor that children were making fun of them. The coach reported that the sizes of shoes on many of the children were either too small or too large for them to participate in physical education, including games.

Betty, a second grade teacher, told of a little girl in her class who fell asleep at her desk; when questioned, she said, "I didn't get much sleep because I had to go sleep on my friend's porch. I didn't want to disturb the people on drugs inside the house. So I just took my jacket and slept in the swing at my friend's, then went home when it got light outside." She further explained that she was very scared by what was happening inside the house. The adults were drinking, dealing drugs, on drugs, and so loud that she was terrified.

As we talked that Tuesday morning, I was aware of real caring on the faces of the teachers. Over the years these dedicated professionals had been spending their own money for clothes, food, and shoes for their poorer children, but with their salaries and families, the amount was very limited.

The teachers shared with me what they knew about the neighborhood and about the hardworking parents who cared for their children and other children as well. As they could, some community grandparents were rearing children who were distant relatives. Over the years some of these grandparents, mostly grandmothers, were the most courageous and self-sacrificing people I had ever met.

This faculty meeting set a series of events in motion. As a faculty we agreed to immediately call our Parent Teacher Association (PTA) board members and lay out the problems with them. I had a meeting with them that afternoon. The president of our PTA had been told of a large department store that advertised for workers to do their yearly inventory over a weekend. She called it and asked if our faculty and parents could volunteer to earn this money. The department store was delighted, and within a few weeks we had twenty-five workers ready for shifts on the weekend planned.

The inventory work proved to be a hoot for all of us. We wore very casual clothes, mostly jeans and tennis shoes, and laughed and counted. We assigned our male coach and male fourth grade teachers to count in the women's lingerie section (they were good sports), and we were convulsed with laughter at all the antics we pulled while doing the work.

Some parents and teachers who could not get away from their homes made us some food and had it brought in. Our faculty and PTA members actually counted inventory for twelve hours a day for three whole days (Monday was a holiday) and got the total inventory done. The inventory process, though tedious and tiring, was fun. The manager enjoyed having such good workers and listening to the bantering among us as we worked.

With this money we were able to purchase a washer and dryer for the school. To solve the body odor and soiled clothing problem, we had teachers send the children to us when they arrived dirty at school. We let them shower or sponge bathe themselves, in the privacy of our clinic bathroom, and put on clean clothes, and then we sent them back to class. During the day we washed their clothes.

When we first started this, we brought donations of clothing from our own homes. Some of our staff members brought in new clothing. Not only would we wash their clothing and give it back to the children, but we would often send the new clothing home. If Louise, the social worker, could not contact the parents, sometimes we would put new sets of clothing on some of the most pitiful children and even new shoes. Then, with notes to the parents that we had washed their clothes and that the new shoes and clothing were free, we would send the children home.

The PTA, faculty, staff, and I were occasionally surprised that this idea did not always help. What we found was that some children came back to school the next day with the old clothes and the old shoes instead of the new ones. I asked Louise to investigate what was happening with these parents. A few desperate parents were actually selling the new shoes and sometimes the new clothes to pay a bill or buy groceries. Sometimes a family member would take the new shoes away from the child and sell or barter them for drugs.

To combat this problem, we worked out a different system for those children. When they came to school we let them take a shower in the clinic, if they were really dirty, and then we loaned them clean clothes and shoes to wear during the day. We washed their dirty clothes while they were at school, and at the end of the day we put their washed clothes back on them to go home. Each day they knew that loaner clothes and shoes waited as soon as they got to school.

A SMALLER BUT IMPORTANT POVERTY ISSUE

While we were in the process of working on the children's cleanliness, I had a visit from two mothers who made an appointment to see me. Their concern was head lice—the risk of their own children getting head lice from other children. Last year several children had head lice, and some parents had become very upset, one of them even to the point of carrying a picket sign outside the front of the school. These two mothers, both white, said that they represented a group of parents who all agreed that the school should have a policy of checking every child once a week for head lice, so as to prevent a general outbreak. They implied that the lice came from African American children.

I told them the school's policy on head lice, a policy widely adopted by elementary schools. When head lice were spotted on a child, we did a check on all the other children in the classroom, the siblings of the child, and any others we believed were in close contact with the child. If any of those had head lice, they were sent home and not readmitted until the lice were gone. I told my visitors that this practice had always been adequate and that I supported it.

The two mothers believed that practice to be inadequate. Said one of them, "There are so many black children in this school that I believe Prescott is at a lot higher risk for head lice than you think. What do you have against a weekly check?"

I explained, "African Americans do not get head lice. That's a fact. Lice only like certain kinds of heads, and none of them are black heads. Head lice do spread because of poor hygiene, and children who don't bathe regularly are most at risk. My reason for opposing a weekly check of every child is because the process would cut too much into our precious time for instruction. Our instruction time is so short, and we have to protect every minute of it."

The mothers left, obviously not sure whether to believe me. As I was coming out of my office two days later, my secretary gave me a distress sign, pointed to a visitor, and said quietly that it was Mr. Mason. He was sitting patiently waiting to see me. I quickly changed direction and had him come in, saying, "Well, Mr. Mason, I am so glad to meet you."

The first day I became principal at Prescott, I had been warned about a Mr. Mason, who was very prejudiced and refused to believe that African Americans do not have head lice. He was nicknamed Mr. H. L. Detective and actually carried a picket sign the year before I arrived about the contamination of head lice. For over two weeks he marched in front of the school, sign about head lice held high. I was warned by my district supervisor to give him anything he wanted should he enter my school concerning checking for head lice. My administrative assistant and secretary had warned me that this was a man to be taken very seriously.

As soon as we entered my office he said, "Well, I just wanted to warn you that I will picket your school if my daughter gets head lice this year as she did last year."

"That is fine; picketing is entirely within your rights as a citizen." This statement just seemed to make him more agitated and angry.

"You don't seem to know who I am," he continued: "Last year I even had the superintendent and school board members down here. I was even pictured in the paper!" Veins began to stand out prominently in his neck.

I said, "Mr. Mason, I really care about your daughter and head lice but am not worried about your picketing the school."

With disbelief in his face, he gasped and turned a dull red: "You mean, you don't care if I picket the school?"

"Not in the least. If it makes you feel better and helps to dissolve some of your anger, I think you should. As a matter of fact, you seem so stressed by this, I feel it probably *is* in your best interest to picket. I really am so worried about you having a stroke that I'll even support you by helping you with your sign. My philosophy is that this strong a reaction to a problem needs an outlet. I would rather you picket than die."

I was very serious, and somehow I conveyed this to Mr. M. With a few words of warning, he left the school. My secretary and clerk had gotten Betsy, and all three were anxiously waiting for me to open the door to see if he would attack me. This is absolutely true, and I was tickled that they cared so much for me. I never saw Mr. M. again.

We did have several cases of head lice that year but never had to check the whole school. I do not remember any child staying out of school more than three days. But one day I did purposely overlook one head lice case for Kevin.

Kevin had been looking forward to the kindergarten field trip to "The Farm" for weeks. He was one of our most disadvantaged children. On the morning of the field trip, his teacher discovered small nits in his head. Resigned to the district rule of a child having to go home immediately, his teacher reluctantly brought him to the office.

"Kevin has head lice, Dr. Lawrence. He can't go with us on the field trip because of this rule that any child with head lice has to immediately go home." Kevin was silently sobbing, tears streaming through the dirt on his face.

Thinking about all he could gain by going on this trip, I said, "Oh, Mrs. Adams, haven't you heard about the latest research on head lice? You can kill head lice in minutes by using a hot hair dryer directly on the hair. [I winked at Mrs. Adams.] I have a hair dryer in my office. After we blow Kevin's hair, then all we have to do is find a baseball hat, cover his head, and he can go!" I directed the two of them to go see the coach. I knew he had some extra donated baseball caps from his T-ball team.

Betsy, always professional and never *publicly* contradicting me, watched this interchange in shocked silence. As the teacher and child hurried off, she quickly followed me into the office, quietly closing the door behind her. "Dr. Lawrence, you have *got* to be kidding. Are you *really* going to let this child go on this trip with a chance that he will infect the whole busload of children?"

I answered, "Kevin has never been out of this town, as far as I know. He lives thirty minutes from the Atlantic Ocean, is six years old, and has never even seen it, and he has never seen farm animals. Going to this farm means a *lot* to him. I'm relatively sure with a cap on he will not give any other children head lice. They only spread by hopping from one head to another. He'll be required to come into my office when he gets back from the farm and stay until school is over. While he's gone, I'll call his mother, and you can get the shampoo from the clinic for him to take home. I will explain the situation to her."

Kevin and Mrs. Adams came proudly back with their trophy, the required baseball cap. I took Kevin into my restroom, turned on the hair dryer, and hopefully *killed* those head lice. I cautioned Kevin, however, that he must not take his cap off at any time while he was on this trip.

I put Kevin on the school bus, emphasizing to Mrs. Adams to keep the cap on at all times. She was all smiles. A few minutes later, as I was meeting with a parent of another child, I glanced up as the bus came by my office. Kevin's face was in the window looking for me. His smile, on a now *clean* face, was ear to ear. He gave me a happy *thumbs up* sign. My heart swelled, and I knew I did the right thing for Kevin and myself! The anxiety I had over breaking the rule lasted for a couple of months, but it was small in comparison. No other cases of head lice appeared in Mrs. Adams's class. The risk had paid off.

THE PROBLEM OF HUNGER

During the time we were working on our clothes and shoes problem, I went to the lunchroom manager, Mr. Miller, and asked him if he had experienced any requests from the children for more food or larger portions. He said, "Every single day! These children are bottomless pits. You just can't fill them up!"

Relieved that they were getting extra food, I said, "Thank goodness, you are giving them extra food within your capability!"

Shocked, he looked at me and said, "I'm not allowed to give any child extra food. We are on a strict budget here, and our portions are dictated by the state and federal government. We are allowed to give the older students a larger portion, but we never give seconds, and no child gets more than any other child."

I told him that I understood but asked about times I had seen food left over in the kitchen and what happened to that food. He said they had to save it to be used with other meals as leftovers or share it among the workers, if the amounts were very small.

In my weekly newsletter to the teachers the next Monday, I asked them to tell me approximately how many children in their classrooms were not getting enough food and to write down their names. They gave me a list of the names within three days, and I was dismayed to find that we had sixty children whom they said were not getting evening meals. When the social worker went to the homes of these children, she discovered that many of them had neither food nor supervision in the evenings. Out of the sixty children listed, she determined who the most desperate and needy were.

A Small Step in Alleviating Hunger

At our next PTA and School Advisory Council meetings, I presented a plan to have an after-school program from 2:00 until 6:00 PM, including an evening meal, for the twenty neediest children. We wanted to have it for all sixty children but knew we did not have the resources for such a large group. The PTA and School Advisory Council agreed, and I started by writing a grant request for funding for the program.

Small grants were available to schools in our district, funded by the businesspeople in our community. The superintendent, as one of his first initiatives to improve schools, established a partnership with the community business leaders. They contributed to a pool of grant moneys. A grant had a maximum of $2,000. We got the maximum $2,000 within a month of our request. I also wrote for another grant for funding from the federal government for $5,000. This would take months to come, but the $2,000 allowed us to get the program started right away.

After we identified the children, we had to get the parents' permission in writing to keep their children from 2:00 to 6:00 PM. The parents also had to agree to pick up the children at 6:00 in the evening. The children absolutely could not come to the program unless the parents picked them up. (We got all the signatures but ended up having to take some of the children home ourselves. We anticipated this, of course, because of the circumstances of these children.)

For additional supplies and moneys, I spoke to the Kiwanis Club, went to the manager of Publix for food donations, and went to the manager of K-Mart for materials. The Kiwanis Club supported the idea and promised to help as it could. One lawyer at that meeting gave me a check for $100. I recognized him as our school board attorney. Another businessman who had a small farm told me of food I could have in the spring if we would come to the farm and pick it. Publix gave me day-old bread and, when we got into a real money crunch, added some staples. K-Mart told me it would hold off on throwing items in the dumpster each month and would call to tell me when to come in. It gave us such things as seasonal display pictures (Halloween, Christmas, President's Day, etc.), extra paper, cardboard, and even usable poster board. With these promises, we began to gather materials and volunteers for the program.

The most important person was someone to plan and cook the meals for twenty children each night. Luckily, Betsy knew of someone in the neighborhood, Mrs. Adams, who had just retired as a lunchroom manager in the district. She was willing to do the job for a salary of $100 a week.

Mrs. Adams also said that she could feed the children on a budget of $100 a week. She bought the food, cooked the meals, and brought them into the school in the evenings. This worked very well. The children had delicious, nutritious meals, such as chicken and rice, great vegetables, and dessert. I did not even consider contacting the health department, as I was required to do. Betsy knew Mrs. Adams personally and could vouch for her cleanliness and her training.

While Betsy and I were making these plans, our social worker, Louise, burst into the office very excited. "Dr. Lawrence, guess what? The school board attorney, without telling anyone, took it upon himself to install a heater in Sandra's house [the child babysitting her siblings at night]! He contacted the utility company, had the heater installed, and named himself responsible for the bill. The grandmother just told me when I went by to check about the children. But she said I must promise not to tell anyone but you because he did not want it known." What a wonderful man! I thanked him very quietly the next time I saw him at a meeting.

THE AFTER-SCHOOL PROGRAM TAKES SHAPE

We had to design the after-school program in sharp contrast to regular school activities, so we would not have burnout on the part of the children. At 2:00 PM the children came in exhausted. So we gave them a good snack first, with juice, and a mat to lie on in the lunchroom; then we ran Bill Cosby videos or other interesting videos while they rested for about forty-five minutes. They were required to relax and just visit or watch the television. Some slept during this time.

Then from 3:00 until about 5:15 PM the children rotated through four different centers. The centers changed every month, but generally they included a creative arts center, a homework center, a sewing center, and a potpourri center. The creative arts center began with each child getting a chance to paint. Later, I remember, we purchased *sun catchers* for the children to paint and take home. The homework center provided assistance and materials for their homework, with a tutor. If they needed to produce a project, using poster board or other materials, these materials were provided by our program.

Another very important center was sewing with Mrs. Adams. After she brought the food in, she taught the children (boys and girls) how to sew hems, put on patches, and do general maintenance of clothes. The children were encouraged to bring in their own clothes to repair. The last center was just called a fun center, and it contained new types of games; fun reading such as comic books and dot-to-dot books; and a large variety of manipulative, educational materials.

After completing the centers, the children were allowed about twenty minutes of free supervised play on the playground before their evening meal. Then at about 5:30 PM, we would help the children clean up the room and wash their hands for dinner. This program became a hit right away with all the children involved.

The program also had a positive effect on the children's self-management that carried over into the classrooms. I remember one specific child named

Yolanda. We nicknamed her (to ourselves) *the belly* because she ate so much. She came to us in kindergarten with no previous school experience or experience with other children except her six siblings. Yolanda was out of control in the classroom. She threw dangerous objects, ran from the teacher, got under desks, and was obnoxious at times. She was tested by our school psychologist and placed part-time with a special learning disability teacher. She also spent time with the guidance counselor.

Because she was identified as one of the twenty neediest children, she began to come to the after-school program. Betsy and I personally spent a lot of time with her individually, helping her work on good social behavior. She truly thrived on the extra food and extra attention, so much so, in fact, that we could use the threat of not letting her stay for the program in the afternoons if she did not show good behavior in school. After three months, Yolanda was able to maintain herself in the classroom and did not have to continue going to the guidance counselor.

The after-school program was a success. We had to have a teacher or administrator on duty every day from 2:00 until 6:00 PM. We had no moneys to pay for anyone to stay after school hours. The faculty and I decided that one teacher would stay with the children one day a month. By using all thirty teachers plus Betsy and me, we could always have someone with Mrs. Adams and the children. This worked fine for about six months, but eventually we only had a few teachers who could stay that late. Because I worked longer hours anyway, I was usually there at least twice a week. Many teachers volunteered as they could.

We had the after-school program for three years before our district adopted an overall after-school program with hired personnel. Before this happened, we had several children who graduated from fifth grade to middle school who had enjoyed the program. Many still wanted to come to the program and be a part of the after-school family. Because most were still slow readers, I knew that having them come to the program and tutor the younger children would also help them in reading. We were able to hire three.

The children who were doing the tutoring were paid 50 cents an hour. This was completely illegal, I found out later. The PTA president and I put our donated moneys into a PTA account that was not governed by the school district, just by the PTA members. So we had no accountability to the district for this money, only to the PTA. I later found out that we were putting the school district at risk because the tutors were not covered by insurance while they were on campus. After I found out about the insurance, we held our collective breath hoping nothing serious would happen. In retrospect, because their tutoring worked so well, I would do it again—somehow.

When these sixth and seventh graders came over to tutor the first, second, and third graders in the program, they loved being called assistant teachers. They tutored during homework time. I also had a chance to keep tabs on the older children's progress.

Several nights we had truly pitiful situations happen when the parents came to pick up their children. Some parents brought their younger children to eat and wanted to eat themselves. This was so sad but we really could not handle the whole neighborhood. We just did not have the funds.

After three years, when our district started funding after-school programs and providing a paid coordinator, we still ran our program as it was originally set up, and I got to hire the coordinator. Our expenses remained nearly the same, however. We still had extra expenses beyond what the district would fund because we had to fund the full meal at night, and we used entirely different materials for the centers in contrast to what the children experienced during the day. Teaching life skills and having many manipulative materials put the materials budget over the amount provided by the district. We continued to solicit donations, and the PTA helped as it could.

THE STORY OF ONE IMPOVERISHED CHILD

We had one particular child who stayed with the after-school program all the years I was at Prescott. He was in the third grade when I came as principal to the school. His mother was a drug addict and prostitute, and his father was in prison. Martin lived at another house filled with drugs at night, and while I was principal, there were four drug busts at his house.

Martin was the first child who came back to us after he went to middle school. He had been of average intelligence in kindergarten through third grade but then got hit by a car, sustained some brain damage, and qualified for disability. He had severe headaches at times, and often he liked to sleep in the clinic after school because his sleep at home was too frequently disrupted. They used all of his disability money for drugs. We kept milk, bread, peanut butter and jelly, and other foods in the refrigerator for him.

I felt strongly that we could make a difference with the children. While I was in my doctoral program, I learned from research that no matter how hopeless a child's home situation is, if he or she has one person who really cares for at least one year, that child has a substantially better chance of making it in life. Seventeen years later Martin is still in my life and calls me every week. He was on disability through high school but decided that he wanted to work instead of stay on disability. He is married now, drives for Pizza Hut, has three children, and reads to his children every day. He is still very limited, but his oldest is in school and doing well.

In a faculty meeting during my last year at Prescott, I told the teachers about mentoring research, lest we feel overwhelmed with our job in helping some of these children. I kept Martin, and fourteen teachers each picked one child who had little chance of becoming productive as an adult without help. I did not follow what happened to these children, but one fifth grade teacher saw her student through paramedic training, and he is functioning well as an adult.

My husband and I recently went to Special Olympics basketball and watched Martin play on his team. He called and invited us to come because it was being held in our city. What a privilege to watch Martin be a star player, interact with his friends and coach, and give us his big smile as he came rushing by!

Martin has been successful because he is a very special person. With a reported IQ of only seventy, he made it through school by having someone who would stay with him. I spoke with his teachers and his principals throughout his school life, even when he moved to other cities and another state. I would always say, "My name is Dr. Lawrence, and Martin Jones is a child I have been working with and looking after for several years. If you have time, could I tell you how special he is?" Without exception, they gave me special help wherever he moved. If I heard from a teacher or counselor that he was not doing his best, I would talk with Martin about it.

Martin lived in Miami, Orlando, and Charlotte, North Carolina. Once or twice I got calls from Miami about Martin being absent. On these occasions, once it was because he could not buy bus tokens to his special school, and another time he did not have shoes. He had to move to several places because he lived with first one cousin for a few months, then another friend, and then another relative.

One day I hope to write his story about the trials and tribulations he went through with no parents. Two stories stand out about Martin. He called me collect every time he called from Miami, and finally I said: "Martin, instead of you calling me collect, how about I send you a phone card, and then I won't have to pay so much money for the calls."

Shocked, he replied, "You are having to pay for these calls? The television says just call 1-800-collect, and I thought that meant it was free."

There are so many poignant and funny stories about Martin trying to break out of the culture of welfare and to survive as an African American who is limited. He has been on Medicaid for his health but for a long time did not know that there were prescriptions that could help with his headaches. There are many, many stories of Martin being taken advantage of because of his good nature and trusting character. He has been repeatedly shortchanged by unscrupulous people who find out that he is not sharp. More often than not, he has learned to call me or my husband for advice about anything he does not understand.

Another story I remember is the time he called and said that his aunt had left him at the bus station in Miami at 8:00 AM in the morning to catch a bus to another town to stay with yet another cousin. Martin had made a mistake: the bus did not leave until 8:00 that night, and he did not have any money or anything to eat. He called me about 5:30 PM. He said, "Dr. Lawrence, I have $23.00 in my bank account, and I have my ATM card, but they told me in the bank to always keep $20.00 in the account, and I am afraid to use my card." I told him to go ahead and use his card for $10.00 and buy himself something to eat. He was so relieved.

I cannot remember the number of times he called me from Miami as a high school student just to talk with me about how good he was being. One night he called and said: "You know I'm not going out after dark because so many teenagers are getting killed or beaten in this neighborhood. So I just don't go out after dark."

"Martin," I said, "that is just so smart. I know it must be hard."

"It sure is because I got a girl I really love, and she loves me, too."

"Martin, I hope you aren't having sex with her. Now you don't need any children before you finish high school."

"No, ma'am, I'm not. She told me she wants to lay with me, but I told her *no* 'cause we aren't on any pills or anything to protect ourselves. And I told her you would kill me if I got a girl pregnant before I finished high school."

Straightforward talk and coaching such as this have helped him manage and make good judgments. My husband and I went to North Carolina to his high school graduation. Martin got a certificate of completion instead of a diploma because he still needs one credit in English. He is still working on his completion.

I know for a fact that Martin is well and happy today, still having a hard time because of his disabilities but functioning nevertheless, because someone took the time to monitor and mentor him. As I write this, we are now proud of the fact that he seldom has to call about problems but, rather, just calls to say hello and that he loves us.

ATTRACTING GOOD TEACHERS TO PRESCOTT

There are a number of hidden barriers to helping children of poverty. One of them surprised me.

Whenever I had a teacher vacancy to fill, I followed the district's procedure of calling the personnel department and requesting interviewees. The district staff screened all applicants who wanted to teach in our district, rating them as to qualifications. I was generally not pleased with the quality of the candidates who were sent to me. Only after a couple of years did I find that the district office staff was sending me none of the teacher candidates who had been rated above average or superior. When I discovered this and called the personnel office about it, I was told that the top teachers did not want to come to schools that serve impoverished areas. After some sleuthing I learned that the district had an unspoken policy of sending the better teacher candidates to the schools serving affluent areas where parents were the most observant and vocal about the quality of teaching. The strategy was to avoid having disgruntled parents.

With this information, I went to the private university located in our town and talked with the head of the education department. I had taught there the summer before I became a principal, so he knew me. I convinced him that my school was the right place to send good and excellent students for their internships.

My reasoning was this: the most common reason a student teacher fails during an internship or has major trouble is a lack of skills in classroom management and discipline. This is also true of experienced teachers whose only experience has been in more affluent schools. They are ill prepared to deal with the poverty and the emotional issues that come up with poor children. They may not know how to communicate well with these children. If teachers are assigned to do their student teaching in these more difficult circumstances, and do well, then they can teach almost anywhere and do fine.

I was finally assigned student teachers from this university. Some of the teachers who interned with us stayed with us and became good teachers at our school. Many wanted to go to other schools. I was never able to reverse the fact that the district sent the most promising, most intelligent (and best looking) candidates to the more affluent schools.

In the next two years, I was able to persuade three of my own special friends, who were teachers elsewhere, to come to Prescott. Then, with the excellent teachers already on staff, we had a small core of superior teachers to bring professionalism at Prescott to a new high. Many are still there today because of what we accomplished and because they believe that these challenging children need the best teachers if they are to have a real chance in society and become the taxpayers and good citizens we need.

6

GETTING RID OF BAD TEACHING AND SUPPORTING GOOD TEACHING

MY HARDEST TASK AS PRINCIPAL

The hardest task I had as principal was concentrating time and energy on evaluating marginal or incompetent teachers at our school and helping them improve or moving them out of teaching. The process of dismissing teachers is different for those with tenure and those without it. Teachers in the first three years of teaching have an annual contract. If they demonstrate incompetence, after getting careful help to improve, they can be fired in any of the three years. Teachers on continuing contract (tenure) can be dismissed only after an extensive plan of dismissal has been followed. It takes hard work that is often stressful for the principal as well as the teacher. Any time I realized that I had to work toward ending a person's career and livelihood, for the sake of the children, was a soul-wrenching time for me. After working extensively with the weak teachers during my first year at Prescott, I felt that the failure of those who did not come up to an acceptable quality of teaching was partly my failure. Fortunately, I had a lot of training and experience that gave me confidence to keep the weeding-out process going.

MY BACKGROUND AS A PROFESSIONAL
REVIEWER PROVES USEFUL

During my fourteen years as a regular classroom teacher, I was grade chair-woman many times and often found myself in the role of helping colleagues on my grade level with discipline and instruction. My last four years in the regular classroom were spent with an added responsibility. I was a professional reviewer for the State Department of Education Professional Practices Council (PPC). The PPC hired highly recommended teachers currently teaching in a regular classroom to be professional reviewers of other teachers regarded as incompetent by their principals. This job involved leaving my classroom for three days and going to another similar classroom, in another school district, and gathering facts about the instruction and discipline in that classroom.

To do this work, I was given specialized training for three twelve-hour days. I learned many techniques of documenting what happens in the classroom. Over the four years I served as a reviewer, I polished my skills as a data gatherer about instruction. Three times I was called as an *expert witness* to testify at a competency hearing about the instruction and discipline in a particular classroom.

Just as importantly, I learned exactly what is required to help a teacher. When a teacher is having problems of any kind in a classroom, there is much assistance given to the teacher from the staff in the school, especially the administration, the school district supervisors, and other teachers in the district. This must all happen before a principal can request a competency review from the State Department of Education.

Over my tenure as peer teacher, curriculum resource teacher, and assistant principal, I worked with over 200 teachers on improving instruction and discipline. So prior to being a principal, I had in my brain a catalog of clues to what was happening in a classroom. I could walk into a classroom and within five minutes tell if the teacher was being effective or not. Over my thirty-two years, I realized that marginal teachers can be sorted into about seven categories:

- good instructional ability but having discipline problems
- good discipline but showing gaps in knowledge in some areas of instruction

- good knowledge of instruction and good discipline but showing little ability to communicate to the children on their level
- good ability but actively disliking some children
- has recognized problems and has practiced, many times for years, covering up problems instead of seeking help (the hardest of all)
- good ability and discipline but lack of commitment to the profession (lazy)

READY TO GIVE ASSISTANCE

By the time my first year as principal was over, I had a very good idea of the instructional strengths and weakness of the faculty. Luckily, Betsy, my administrative assistant, who had a classroom to handle the year before, was assigned as a full-time assistant to me. She was a wonderful first grade teacher, and I hated to lose her in first grade but was thrilled to have her full-time.

Because the whole faculty now knew what I expected for evaluations and had exact guidelines for reading, I knew that I could spend more time during the second year assisting in the classrooms and really attacking the serious problems. My office staff was very committed and helpful and tried very hard to let me have at least two hours a day in the classrooms and sometimes more. Some days, however, Betsy and I had so many administrative duties and meetings that neither of us could be in the classrooms, sometimes for as long as a week.

MAKING A LIST OF PRIORITIES

Betsy and I had several conferences to decide a strategy. We wanted to help all our teachers, and I needed to start documenting and assisting, intensely, those who I felt might actually be damaging children because of their weaknesses in instruction. We talked about all the teachers and what I had discovered about their teaching. Because Betsy had been at Prescott for twenty years, several as administrative assistant, she also knew a lot about the strengths and weakness of these teachers. Betsy and I decided that we would alternate our times in the classrooms, to have an administrator available at all times.

Though we wanted to spend the most time with the teachers we suspected were marginal or incompetent, we would visit all of the teachers—so as not to appear to be targeting any of them and to show evenhanded support. We decided that I would tackle the most difficult teachers. These teachers were the ones who I thought might be incompetent. Betsy would help in the primary grades with marginal teachers in reading instruction and do demonstration teaching about discipline and instruction as needed.

During the first six weeks of school, I visited several teachers' classrooms, sometimes for several hours at a time. I wanted to give good support to my excellent teachers just by helping with teaching a reading group or reading to the children.

CLASSROOM VISITATIONS

My first classroom visit was with a fifth grade veteran teacher. I knew that she had an exceptional record for effective instruction and discipline. I stayed with her for three hours and was truly amazed at her rapport with her students. She absolutely treated them as responsible and capable and had a minimum of distractions from any kind of disruption. I never heard her raise her voice. Her teaching style was strongly motivational, moving at a rapid pace, with not one minute lost. As she and her class were lining up to go to lunch, she had them spelling words as they got in line. I was truly amazed at all she was able to teach in the time allotted and asked for a conference with her that afternoon.

"Linda, my visit with you this morning was sheer pleasure. You are without a doubt one of the best teachers I have ever observed. Tell me a little about your ability to control the children and have them focus on you and listen so well. I watched the clock, and you had virtually no downtime for discipline problems."

"Well," she said, "I always spend the first six weeks training the children to work well in my classroom. My system for teaching students to be self-managing has three key principles behind it. One is that *telling* and *explaining* the good behavior patterns I want them to adopt is not enough. For our population of students I have to give them something for the good behavior. The second principle to keep in mind is that I am helping them move to the place where the good behavior is automatic and becomes its own reward.

"The third principle is that everyone controls their own behavior. I say to my students, 'Your behavior is under your control. Not the teacher's. I can't control your behavior. The only person that can do that is you. What I can do is provide a big payoff to you for good behavior. And I can make sure there are consequences when behavior doesn't meet expectations.'

"What I do is award students points for good behavior, and the points go into a pool to earn the class a big payoff. I have chosen seven categories to judge behavior:

Enter (the classroom)
Focus
Volume
Movement
Neatness
Cooperation
Exit

"I constantly refer to these during the day, rewarding the behaviors I see. I arbitrarily assigned a number of points to each category."

"Linda," I said, "would you mind explaining a couple of the most important categories in detail for me, so I can get an idea of your system?"

"I'll be glad to, but all the categories are essential. The first day in the classroom, I explain the categories to them and show them the chart I leave up for them explaining again each category, so they refer to the chart frequently.

"I begin on the first morning by telling them about earning points for the class for the seven categories. For example, I tell them, 'For *Entry*, to earn two points you have to come into the room quickly, quietly, and efficiently. You have to pick up your folders of work from yesterday and correct mistakes for the first few minutes of class. I will leave you notes on your papers, and you have fifteen minutes. If there are no corrections, you may choose something from the *Children's Fun Box* for extra credit.'

"Sometimes coming in quietly is not that easy because they have to walk up a long metal ramp to the portable and everyone wants to stomp their feet. But all I say to them when they are noisy, 'Oops, that wasn't a two-point entry. Maybe tomorrow you will do better.' Then the next day, I meet them before they come up the ramp, remind them of the rules again, and then praise them highly if they do what they are supposed to do. Sometimes this is a time to give an extra point if I can't even hear their feet.

"I have to spend a lot of time the first six weeks, taking time to mark the points immediately on a graph as they happen in all categories.

"*Focus*, the second category, means everybody has to look and listen to me when I am teaching. Of course, I tell them that when they pretend they are listening, that works. But when I call on them for the answer and they don't know what I am talking about, they are not focused. If I call on a child and he or she says, 'Huh?' the student loses focus points for the class. The child can say, 'I don't understand,' or give me the wrong answer, as long as he or she is with me and knows what I am talking about.

"*Volume* means I expect the children to talk to one another but in a moderate voice, pose questions, and turn to their neighbor to discuss the answer. I give them enough time to do that and then I ask for their answers. So they have to talk to each other and discuss solutions. In independent centers it is understood that I expect them to be talking quietly with their neighbors and working through the problems. Their volume for the day can earn four points.

"*Movement* is when I tell the students, 'When you move around the classroom there is no pushing, shoving, or not giving enough space for a student.' Their movement can earn four points.

"*Neatness* means they have to leave the centers as neat as they found them. They have to push the chairs back into place where they are supposed to be. One of our science centers is about studying volume. We cannot have water in the portable to do this, so we use rice. Sometimes there is an accident, and they spill the rice, but they have to be responsible and clean up after themselves when that happens. They earn four points for neatness.

"*Cooperation* is a big item, so I put a premium number of six points on that.

"*Exit* is when I dismiss everybody after debriefing, they close up for the day, and we are having our dismissal; they have to return their folders and their pencils to me in an orderly way. They can earn twenty-eight points a week if they are perfect in all areas.

"I tally the points for the class each day and record them on a class behavior graph. Data analysis is a big strand we are working on in math, so it fits in well with that study. When the class earns a certain amount of points (at the discretion of the teacher), I allow the class one hour of games and popcorn. This is a nice opportunity for me to get to teach the math games that I don't have time for in the regular classroom day. The children love the games, and they count for instructional time.

"It's really easy to say, 'Oh, let's focus on the positive behavior,' but let me tell you they really know how to push your buttons. Now if you get really angry, and just start taking away points, and show frustration with their behavior, you have lost the battle. You will have undone a lot, and you have to roll back up and start over. That is very, very hard to do. So you have to resist going overboard with anger. When you are angry, if you possibly can, look around and see what good is happening. Comment on the good behavior of another student and ignore, as much as you can, negative behavior.

"I notice that new teachers are learning more about discipline in their college work. They remember what they learned but have little practice. They don't know the pitfalls. When I hear a teacher say, 'You've lost ten points for the class, you little monster,' she is just hurting her credibility. She needed to walk away from it and come back and really, really look for something positive with a child nearby. The whole idea is keeping the disrespectful child in the herd. Staying on their case constantly takes them out of the herd of the class. It is very important that they feel welcome in the classroom at all times. Kind of look for that thing that gets them back into the group. The important thing, for all the students, is to identify, by giving out points, that they are connecting to a certain behavior you want."

I said: "So to the class you don't say, 'That was another point.' You say, 'That was a good entry, that was a three-point entry.' Identifying for them what they have done right and that what you want them to do is important. They really know when they are doing something wrong, so you don't have to focus on that."

"Yes," she replied, "what's really nice about this program is it makes a smooth transition to self-management. As you get into the year, you forget to give the points or they forget to ask you for the points. Their behavior starts to become its own reward."

I thanked Linda and once again emphasized how much I appreciated her and her view of strategies to use with discipline. I emphasized that I was eager to support her in her teaching with resources, if she lets me know.

Linda's approach would not suit every teacher. It is one good model, but each teacher has to find what works for him or her and be consistent with it every day and all day.

That day I visited another good teacher, who loved to play the piano at break times and sing with the children. This was especially comforting to me because I always loved singing in my first and second grade classrooms. We would march around the room, singing at the top of our lungs, and a lot of tension was released. This teacher was a good second grade teacher, and I enjoyed the visit. I found no problems with instruction and determined that she was a good teacher—another one to whom I could simply give support as she requested it.

JANET

The previous year, in the spring, one of the school board members asked me what I was going to do about Janet Anderson. I said, "Well, I am in all the classrooms right now just finding out what we need to do to improve instruction." He said, "She has been at that school for fifteen years, and many people know she doesn't know how to teach, but no one has ever done anything about her."

I said, "Well, Dr. Johnson, have former principals known about her?"

He answered in the affirmative.

"Then, why do *you* think nothing has ever been done about her?" He answered, in a reflective, halting way, "The thing about Mrs. Anderson is that she is so sweet and so good. All the children just love her; the faculty loves her. She has had a really hard life, being left with two daughters and one son to rear alone, and she retires in about five years." I promised Dr. Johnson that I would give Janet the same due process that every teacher is entitled to have and would look into the situation carefully.

I then went on to tell him about the dedication I saw at Prescott among the faculty. I said, "Whether instructionally competent or not, I am witnessing at least 50 percent of the teachers coming to school almost at dawn and staying until almost dusk. Then they leave their classrooms with a burden of student papers to grade at home. Often I see a teacher holding the hand of a child to take home because he or she worked with the child after school time. All teachers have a certain degree of this dedication. For an average salary (in our district) of less than $29,000 a year, they give more than any other kind of profession I can think of. Obviously, the joy of working with children is what keeps most of them so dedicated. Mrs. Anderson, daily, has former students come to her room after school just to give her a hug before they go home. Did you know that teachers have to plan ahead many hours to be on target in the classroom? Teachers spend several hours planning for each subject, every day."

Dr. Johnson replied, "Well, I know from being on the school board for years that overall our teachers and staff really do have this kind of dedication to children. I see it when I visit every school. To hear you report specifically about what you have seen at Prescott just helps me see they need to get more appreciation for their work."

I thanked him and said that I would get back to him about Mrs. Anderson. I already had Janet Anderson as one of my priorities.

CALLING A SCHOOL BOARD MEMBER TO BE ADMINISTRATOR

Two weeks ahead of time I made a schedule with Janet to observe her. I planned to spend the whole day with her, as I knew Betsy was supposed to be available on that date to monitor the campus. That weekend Betsy had a family emergency and would be gone the whole week. Because I knew the teacher had made preparation for my visit, I hated to cancel. So I decided to go ahead with my plans if I could get the school board member, Dr. Johnson, to come take over the campus for me.

"Hi, Dr. Johnson, this is Carolyn Lawrence. Do you remember our conversation about a teacher you thought might be incompetent?" He rather hesitantly said, "Yes." "Well, I really need to spend an entire day with her on Thursday, and Betsy, my assistant, has to be out of town next week for a family emergency. Would you consider coming to our school and being our 'principal' for a day?"

Dr. Johnson was a college professor and very much a gregarious risk taker. I could tell that he was pleased to be asked when he said, "Well, certainly, I think I could do that. I used to love to work in the schools before being a college professor. What would you want me to do?"

I replied, "I need for you to handle discipline problems that come to the office and just be available around the campus. If you could come by any afternoon before next Thursday, we can walk the campus, and I will show you our general

routines. I will give you a copy of our lunchroom schedule, our discipline program, and other routines about the day, and you and I would just pretend I was
not on the campus. When you are here on Thursday, if you would just keep a log
of what happens if you have anything you think I especially need to know and
just have someone come and get me if things get into a bind. Otherwise we will
go over everything at the end of the day. I cannot tell you how much this will
mean to me, and I think the teachers and children will enjoy having you here."

I knew he was pleased when I saw him at a school board meeting the following evening, and he was telling several people about being my principal
for a day. He was also saying what a good way it was for school board members to see what was happening in the schools and keep more in touch.

So as not to raise faculty concerns about Janet, Betsy and I told the faculty that Dr. Johnson wanted to visit the school and see what it would feel
like to be in the principal capacity. In having Dr. Johnson substitute for me
for a day while I was with a teacher, we want to give the impression that my
spending a day in a classroom was just routine and did not imply that any
particular teacher was especially targeted. The superintendent thought that
this was a great idea and began to have visions of all district staff and board
members helping the principals for one day during the year.

This marginal, possibly incompetent, kindergarten teacher was one of the
sweetest teachers on our faculty. She was a wonderful person, a great har-
monizer on the faculty, and never had anything but good to say about anyone. She had many admirable qualities. Other teachers on campus, I noticed, came to her for advice about discipline. Janet came to me twice when
two of her fellow kindergarten teachers had terrible discipline problems and
volunteered to have those children transferred to her class. Within one
month she had both of these children completely under control and happy.
At faculty meetings, many times she would put faculty members at ease over
a problem by coming up with a compromise solution that worked for us all.

The children adored her, and she was a mother to many children who had
no mothers at home for them. Many older children stopped by on their way
home to give her a hug.

Although I suspect the teachers who had been at Prescott many years
knew she might have some teaching problems, I never heard one word of
criticism. The entire faculty seemed to want to look after her and protect her
however they could.

The first time I spotted a problem in Janet's teaching was during the Open House at the first of the year. Children's papers were on their desks that night for the parents to review. I stopped by the room and saw on some desks some comments written by Janet with glaring grammatical errors. I was horrified. The more I worked with Janet during the year, the more I realized that she was very limited in what she knew.

In my daylong visit in her class, I saw exemplary rapport with her children and wonderful life values in her teaching. These values seemed to come effortlessly in her conversations with the children. I began to wonder if there was any way to keep her as a teacher other than for kindergarten. She did have good foundation skills of teaching colors, numbers, storytelling, sequencing, and other prekindergarten skills.

Even though I saw her serious limitations, I still could not see Prescott without her. My first priority, however, was always the children, so I had a real dilemma.

Betsy and I started thinking about how we could deal with Janet and, at the same time, not damage the children's instruction in any way. Luckily, in about two weeks—a godsend—we qualified for a preschool program. We were to select twenty children from poverty homes who were deemed most likely to not make it in school. These four-year-old children would work for a year on readiness skills for reading and counting. Some skills included recognition of colors, letters, and numbers; being able to listen carefully; and learning to know how to talk in complete sentences. The teacher would read to them several times a day and teach them to enjoy listening to good stories and nursery rhymes. She would also teach them that reading is communication through words. Just as important, they were to absorb skills for functioning well in a group of peers.

We were given this program because we served a low-income area. I knew that there would be money allotted for the materials in the program. If we were going to keep Janet, this was possibly an avenue. Janet already knew that she needed much improvement in her instruction. By this time in the school year we had already had many conversations, and I had been in her room a lot. I knew of materials to buy and could help her with her lesson plans. I thought Janet would be glad for the input from me about the toys, games, songs, and other instructional materials.

When I approached her about this program, she was very hesitant and skeptical. She did not want to change grade levels, but I think she knew that

I was giving her a choice in order not to start dismissal proceedings. I gave her many positive strokes about her contributions to the faculty and truthfully managed to tell her that she would be doing me a favor.

She agreed, and I was relieved because I knew that with careful guidance and assistance, Janet was just what these children needed. We would have the opportunity to work with her. I would meet with her to order materials, make weekly lesson plans, and do demonstrations. Also, I could hire an aide to be with her—a very bright parent I knew and trusted.

The aide I had in mind very much wanted a job in the school, had been volunteering at the school for a long time, was well educated, loved Janet as a person, and was one of our PTA board members. She was thrilled with this opportunity of helping to mold this new classroom.

Janet took some additional training in preschool education and truly turned into a good preschool teacher. Betsy and I met frequently with her and helped in the classroom. We knew we had the backup of this good aide, who turned out to be an exceptional person who helped me in many ways. And within one year, Janet not only was competent in this area but also was really admired and appreciated for how she made these children grow.

MY MOST PROBLEMATIC TEACHER

The teacher who gave me the most problems was the media center specialist. Her main problem, which literally drove me to distraction, was that she did not like children. She had been at the school for over thirty years, was sure that principals come and go, and believed that her domain could never be challenged or changed.

Other than reading stories to the children and allowing them to check out books, with a certain amount of disdain, she thought the media center was her private sanctuary. She did not ever want children to spontaneously browse when interested in a topic. I wanted an individual, a small group, or a whole class to use the center at what the teacher thought was a *teachable moment.* When a child or a class becomes truly excited about learning a particular subject, that is the crucial time for seeking and finding the resources they need—instantaneously if possible.

You will remember that during the past school year, I had worked with the media specialist repeatedly, even to the point of giving her one of my four-hour office aides from the office staff. This was to ensure that she had adequate help for what I wanted her to do.

Because of Mrs. Chance's status in the community, no one had approached her to monitor what she was doing in the media center. During the past year, I noticed few teachers or students using the media center. I got so discouraged that at one point I asked Mrs. Chance to go to the teachers' classrooms and ask them what resources she could provide for their curricula. This, I observed, she did in a halfhearted way, but I saw no increase in teacher use.

I spent one day with her trying to set up our computers in the media center. She had not uncrated them and had no clue about how to use them. She did not know the other media equipment well enough to help the teachers use it. I could not believe it! Most teachers depend on the media specialist to assist with video recording and production, new machines, and new technology, and we had new equipment not being used. I felt that she was not enthusiastic about learning because she had asked for no help from the district staff to train her.

I contacted the district media supervisor and told her of the problems I was having. She had warned me about Mrs. Chance's performance in the beginning. I asked her to come out and spend a day with Mrs. Chance. This would be part of my documentation on her that would help me build a case for improvement or dismissal.

Of course, Mrs. Chance swelled up with hostility toward me, which went mostly undetected because nobody on the staff had seen her any other way. The district media specialist, with a month's advance notice, came out and spent a day with her.

The specialist sent me a report about a week later and actually told me that she could not find anything seriously amiss, that Mrs. Chance seemed to be working to capacity, and that, yes, there were a few inadequacies but nothing she could call evidence of incompetence. To support her opinion that she was not incompetent, she sent me a copy of Mrs. Chance's annual report—a form that media specialists send directly to the district office. Among other things, it showed very high circulation from Prescott's lending library.

Needless to say, after my talks with the district person and my experiences with Mrs. Chance, I was dumbfounded, but I realized that visiting her for one day, it is hard to tell exactly what is happening. After Mrs. Chance got a copy of the supervisor's letter, she settled down even more into the old routine, and the media center was virtually empty all the time. I went in for a meeting with Mrs. Chance.

"Mrs. Chance, I know you have read the report from the district media specialist. She does state that you have some inadequacies that need correcting. These will have to be corrected, and I have made you a list of my priorities, which include the following:

- Welcome children who come to the media center in such a way that they are happy when they leave and are eager to come back.
- Communicate with each teacher, individually, at least once every two weeks.
- Show me a log at the end of each month noting when you had contact with a teacher.

"This is all I want us to have as goals for this month and next month, and step by step, we will see if I might be able to detect more communication going on with the teachers and children."

"Dr. Lawrence, I don't know where you get the idea that the children or teachers don't like to come to the media. These teachers and I have been friends for years, and we have a wonderful relationship."

Frustrated, I said, "Let's do this, Mrs. Chance. I want to close the media center for two days next week, and I would like you to visit my former school and see another type of media center. Maybe you will like what they are doing, and you can also give them some of your ideas."

She agreed to do this, and I was excited to call my former colleagues in the media center at Ancient Oaks Elementary. They agreed to show Mrs. Chance how to use new technology and how an open scheduling media center works. They looked forward to helping me if they could. Also, sending her there would be evidence that I had given her opportunities to see excellent examples of what I expected of her—evidence that could be used in making a case for incompetence.

When Mrs. Chance returned, she came immediately to my office. "Dr. Lawrence, I want you to know the media center at Ancient Oaks has an entirely different situation than at Prescott. They have *two* full-time media specialists *and* an aide, so they can do *much* more than I will ever be able to do."

I replied, "I can see why you would think that, but you need to remember they have over 1,200 students at Ancient Oaks. We have about 480. I just wanted you to get an idea of some new ideas that you may like."

"Well, I did like some of their ideas, but don't see how I can implement any of their ideas without much more help. I think I am really doing a more-than-adequate job here a Prescott."

"Mrs. Chance, I know you have told me that I just don't see what is going on and don't realize how many children come into the media. But I will not rest until we have more action in the media center."

By this time, I was completely frustrated with Mrs. Chance and wondered how I was ever going to make a case for her dismissal. I talked this over with Betsy, and she was just as perplexed. I decided that her circulation reports were one avenue I could explore for discrepancies because I knew the reports to the district office sounded false. But how was I going to prove this?

I decided that during Christmas break, when I was on duty but teachers were not, I would investigate the circulation reports. I spent hours looking at checkout dates on individual books (we did not have computer checkout then). I wrote down the last circulation date on over 1,000 books, a sampling of every tenth book.

If the books were being checked out as she reported to the district, then the dates and sign-outs of the books would reflect this. Of the checkout dates I found in the backs of the books, 87 percent were from the late 1960s through the 1970s, with 13 percent checkouts being in the 1980s. Clearly, Mrs. Chance was tremendously exaggerating her circulation reports to the district office, which is, of course, a serious offense.

After Christmas, I called my district supervisor and reported this to him. He was already familiar with what had happened previously. I also called the district media supervisor and asked her how long books are allowed to be on the shelves without being checked out and replaced with new books. She told me that books are purged every two years. If a book has not been checked out for over two years, then that book is replaced with a new book reflecting new trends. Mrs. Chance's report of how many books she had purged each year was inconsistent with what I found. So from this information I realized that Mrs. Chance not only was padding the circulation but also was not purging old books.

I did know that she had some new books on the shelves because at the beginning of my first and second years I gave her particular titles I wanted her to order. They were mostly what I had researched or experienced with children in the fiction section. She was responsible for updating atlases, the history section, and the nonfiction selection with up-to-date current titles.

So I asked her to report for a conference with me after school. "Mrs. Chance, I asked you to come in today to tell you of a very disturbing problem I found over the holidays. I personally did a random sample of over 1,000 books in the media center to check circulation. I found a large discrepancy between what you have been reporting to the district office and what I discovered.

"First of all, you have books that haven't been checked out since the 1960s, and you know that books not checked out in two years are to be purged. Here is my list of titles and dates from the random sample I did. I talked with your supervisor, and she said your reports reflect that you have done the purging. Second, the ratio of what you are reporting as circulation and my random sample of 1,000 out of our 10,000 books, fiction and nonfiction, shows that you have been padding your circulation reports to the district.

"Now, as far as I am concerned, you have two choices. You can resign after this year, with your thirty years in the district, and I will gladly have us plan a big retirement party for you, or I can call in the State of Florida Professional Practices Council [PPC] to confirm what I have found."

I watched her face while I was speaking. At first I saw fury and hostility, but by the time I had finished talking she had lost all color in her face and was visibly shaken. She just stared at me in disbelief, and I did not know exactly what that meant. So I said, "You let me know, after you have investigated your rights, gone to your union representative, and taken as much time as you need to decide what you want to do. Those alternatives are the only two I am offering to you. I will need to know your decision within three weeks because calling in the PPC is a somewhat time-consuming process. Here is a pamphlet for teachers explaining exactly what happens when they send in a reviewer. Whoever they send in will be a media specialist, currently working in a school similar to ours, with as close to the same circumstances as you have. The reviewer is told nothing ahead of time and comes completely unbiased to collect data for three days with you. I am not allowed to tell the reviewer anything about you and just let her make her own decision about whether you are competent. Then you are allowed a hearing, and I will testify, without the reviewer hearing me at all. The reviewer then testifies, and a decision is made. So the review is completely fair."

Without saying a word, she left the office, and I went back to my other duties. Within a week, she came into my office one morning and told me that she had decided to resign rather than have a battle with me, but she wanted me to understand that I was pushing her out unfairly.

I complimented her for her years of service, and I told her that I would let her tell people why she was resigning and that I would not ever reveal our conversations. Mrs. Chance told me that she would like to have a retirement party and that she would give me a list of whom to invite. I promised her that at the party I would praise her for the years she had committed to the district.

When she left my office, I felt a tremendous amount of sadness for her and relief that I would not have to take this any further. But I felt little joy over having to force this woman out of her livelihood.

In the meantime, I had many more responsibilities and many more teachers to visit. Betsy and I conferred often, made a chart of all the teachers, and checked to be sure that we were fairly distributing our time among the classrooms.

This second year was very exciting. The teachers and I were thrilled with the progress we were making. We were mostly a very happy family and began to do some social outings and parties. I do not think I had any faculty members who did not come to the occasional get-together, with the exception of Mrs. Chance.

Betsy and I were extremely busy all the time. Our parents really began to support us in most areas. We still had some occasional incidents that were a real test of patience and creativity.

WORKING WITH AVERAGE TO MARGINAL TEACHERS

We had several teachers who just needed prodding in certain ways, and as I discovered what they needed to improve their instruction, Betsy and I pitched in to help. One teacher had been in the school for many, many years, and her room was cluttered with old materials and did not look cheerful or clean. I got her a substitute, and together we cleaned the room, went over old files and threw out most of them, and redid the bulletin boards. She was a good teacher, loved the children, and did not recognize the deterioration of the room. She appreciated the help. I had maintenance paint the room over the holidays.

Mrs. Sweet was a reasonably good teacher, was a little too strict with the children, and had an attractive room, but gave students too much paperwork. Instead of having the children enjoy learning by having them write on the chalkboard or use our supply of manipulative materials for practicing skills, to learn in concrete ways, she just gave the children paper after paper to either color, practice their work, or complete preprinted assignments.

She also relied almost exclusively on the textbooks, with little variety or hands-on learning. I remember one particular day when she was having a science lesson and I was in the class. She was teaching the children the parts of a plant: roots, stem, petals, and flowers. As the children were looking at the picture in the science book, I said, "Mrs. Sweet, do you think we might go outside and find real plants that have roots, stems, petals, and flowers?" She quickly agreed, and we all had a good lesson outside—which took a little more time than reading from the science book.

I also worked with her and helped her by bringing in manipulative materials for multiplication facts practice and language skills that the children needed to practice. They could practice on their own level with the manipulatives instead of all using the same printed exercises. The children's favorite was *Step Manipulatives for Children* (P. O. Box 337, Mukilteo, WA 98075; 800-225-7837). I still find these materials very helpful today when I tutor. These recommendations are completely from my experience; I have nothing to gain from the sale of these materials.

Another problem I encountered was with two teachers of the Educable Mentally Handicapped. When they talked about their children, I noticed an attitude of resigned acceptance that their children could not learn much. That attitude bothered me a lot because I knew they were otherwise satisfactory teachers.

So Betsy and I talked with the teachers about the importance of the children's self-esteem. The teachers agreed to introduce some of our new manipulative materials into the classrooms and match them to the skill levels of the children. Working with the matched materials would help them have successes every day—which should help their self-image as learners. We worked with the two teachers during a teacher workday and helped establish centers with manipulatives for the range of instructional levels they had in their rooms. The teachers gave the students the "Coopersmith Self-Esteem Inventory," and we decided to re-administer it at the end of the year to see if the students showed gains.

I went into the classrooms and taught one day for each teacher, showing them how I would interject positive self-esteem statements into my teaching: "Are you smart, or what?"; "I am so pleased with the way you are taking care to write clearly"; and "I can really tell you are trying, and that is what is so important."

The self-esteem inventory showed most of their students having very low self-esteem. At the end of the year, in the two classes, there were only three children who were still having self-esteem problems. I believe that some of this was because they were in the special class and knew that the other students in the school recognized them as labeled. Subsequently, the next year we placed these children into regular classrooms except for reading and math instruction.

One third grade teacher, who was a member of a clique of status leaders in the school, was very lazy and only mediocre in her teaching. She had the ability to be a top-notch teacher but admitted that she only wanted to get on a continuing contract (tenure) this year and then use teaching as a backup if her other career did not work. She was in the third year of her contract, and I had to decide whether to give her a continuing contract or not. Not doing so would mean that she could no longer teach in this school.

I went to her and talked with her about her potential and what I expected. Because she was a member of this group at the school that had always had preferential treatment from the previous principal, she thought that her continuing contract status was secure. I understand why the former principal had liked this group. They were all good teachers and enthusiastic workers. The exception was this third grade teacher who did not want to do the work.

At the end of the year, I did not put this teacher on continuing contract because she refused my help and had not done what we had worked out for her to do to improve. Although I knew that this would cause a major division between some of my best people and me, I could not in good conscience give this teacher a lifetime contract to do mediocre work.

NEGATIVE ATTITUDES ON CAMPUS

Because I did not give the third grade teacher a continuing contract, the new school year started with four of my best teachers and one secretary showing open hostility to me on the campus. This became so blatant at the first of the year that I even had to call these people in and tell them that they were on taxpayers' time and that they must not speak negatively at school in front of parents, children, or other teachers.

They took this meeting as a challenge to discredit my principalship and to be as uncooperative as possible. To make a long story short, I had several visits with the president of the teachers' union, always stayed within the bounds of professionalism, and ultimately traded teachers with other principals. With the help of principal friends, my secretary was moved to the district office to work and two teachers were traded to other schools.

In any school, there comes a time when the principal has to confront hostility. There are negative comments made occasionally, I guess, about every principal. But the campus climate is ultimately affected by people who persist in negative talk and activity, and the climate they create is draining to everyone. I would not tolerate this even for a short period of time. I gave these people several chances to improve, but when I saw that there was a permanent chasm between us, I knew that even though they were good teachers and a great secretary, they had to change or leave. They chose to leave. I was sorry to lose such good people but knew that the children's best interests, once again, had to be the first priority.

MY EXCEPTIONAL KINDERGARTEN TEACHER

I would like to end this chapter with the story of my all-time favorite kindergarten teacher. When I walked into her classroom, I saw children working in centers on handmade manipulatives to learn skills concretely instead of just using paper and pencil. There were about 150 *work jobs* in the centers. One example is small garages made of milk cartons, covered with contact paper, with dots on top for quantities. Small cars with numbers on them from one dot to ten dots sat in a line in front of the garages.

Each child had a record sheet, and each work job had a number. The teacher or a volunteer initialed the child's form when a work job was successfully completed. This information was then reported to the parents. The teacher had a list of work jobs by name and description that was sent home several times that year.

I saw in the children such constructive energy and love of school in completing these tasks. When I asked her about this, the teacher told me: "These ideas are from a book by Addison-Wesley entitled *Work-Jobs*. My friend and I did not have money to buy the materials, so we went and bought the book and made the materials during the summer. My friend and I worked all summer. We should have bought stock in contact paper. We used to cover everything in order to preserve our efforts. The paper also made them as child-proof as possible, and we saved the materials in boxes that were also covered in contact paper."

I am sorry to say that I only had this teacher for two years before she was recognized by the district as one of the most outstanding teachers of kindergarten and became a curriculum resource person. She subsequently helped hundreds of teachers and children and was and is still an inspiration.

Over the six years I was principal at Prescott Elementary, I was able to get thirteen continuing contract teachers who were incompetent, or marginal but refused to take steps to improve, out of education entirely. I did transfer one marginal teacher, though not without warning the receiving principal.

My goal when I came to Prescott was not to get anyone out of the field of education or to take anyone's job, but it was to improve instruction in our school. On a personal basis, I knew and loved each of these teachers as people, and I believe that most respected and loved me. But in the end, as it must be, schools exist not for the teachers but for the children and their best interests, period.

7

REFLECTIONS

MY MISTAKES

- Making every staff member a friend, learning about their personal lives, and trying to help with their problems. This was a major mistake because their problems weighed me down professionally. I also knew my incompetent and marginal teachers' families and still had to get rid of these people. If I could do it over, I would treat them all warmly as professional colleagues and not build personal relationships.
- Being a crusader in the district as an advocate for the children of all schools and bucking the district staff. Although I think I did much good with discussions and arguments with district staff about policies that I saw as against the best interests of children, I believe now that I would only buck the system on behalf of my own school. When you try to change long-standing district policies, you create a lot of animosity at the district level toward yourself, and that means painful repercussions. If I could do it over, I would quietly run my school contrary to policies when needed and let our outcomes show the merits of our alternative way.

- I would go much slower in deciding my strategies, as the research says. I would take more time and gather much more data before suggesting any substantial change. I did not take time to recognize all the good things my teachers were doing before I started telling them about teaching methods supported by research. I could have found in their classrooms many strategies consistent with the research and used these as good examples. That approach would have given me a solid base of rapport with the teachers—a platform from which to introduce new things.

MY MAIN SUCCESSES

- Implementing a reading program that made every child successful in reading over the six years I was at the school. Many did not attain the level they needed, but all made major progress.
- Creating a positive campus where children wanted to come to school, where they came to me with their problems, and where our attendance level was very high. Because of the positive strict discipline and fair rules, teachers and children alike felt respected.
- Implementing and maintaining an after-school program that continues today throughout the district. It was and is an integral part of the success of the most disadvantaged students.
- Coaching many principal interns in our district, for six-week periods, about the practical applications of research in curriculum and instruction. Most are principals today.
- Mentoring many children and seeing them thrive. But in particular staying as friend and helper to one troubled boy from age seven until today. He is now twenty-four and coping well with life—and we still talk every week.
- Having a wonderful, exciting, exhilarating time for six years. These were the most challenging and rewarding years of my career as an educator (so far).

ABOUT THE AUTHOR

Carolyn McKenzie Lawrence was an elementary school teacher, reading supervisor, curriculum resource teacher, assistant principal for instruction, and elementary principal for thirty-two years. Born in Atlanta, Georgia, she is one of five daughters. While working full-time, she completed her undergraduate degree at Georgia Teachers College in 1962, her graduate degree at Rollins College in 1976, and her doctorate at the University of Florida in 1984.

In 1964 she was nominated for "Outstanding Teacher of the Year" in Huntsville, Alabama. In 1966, she became a reading supervisor for a county in Alabama. She was named to the Professional Practices Council in Florida in 1973, was "Principal of the Year" in her school district in 1987, and was named one of "Five Outstanding Educators" in 1989 by the National Parent Teacher Association. She has been a member of Phi Delta Kappa, the Association for Supervision and Curriculum Development, the National Education Association, and the National Association of Elementary School Principals. Lawrence now lives in Florida and especially enjoys tutoring children with reading problems.